THE SUNDAY TIMES
Education Online

Matthew Wall

HarperCollins*Publishers*

Matthew Wall is a freelance journalist and TV researcher/producer best-known for his weekly *Web Wise* internet column in *The Sunday Times*. He also writes internet features for the paper's Doors section and has written several internet reports for business. He also advises companies on web design and strategy.

HarperCollins Publishers
77–85 Fulham Palace Road
Hammersmith
London W6 8JB

fireand**water**.com
Visit the book lover's website

First published 2001

Reprint 10 9 8 7 6 5 4 3 2 1 0

© Times Newspapers Ltd 2001
The Sunday Times is a registered trademark of
Times Newspapers Ltd.

ISBN 0 00 710241-0

Designer: Sylvie Rabbe
Editor: Sarah Barlow

Designed, edited and typeset by Book Creation Services Ltd.

Printed in Great Britain by Omnia Books Ltd, Glasgow G64.

Acknowledgments

I would like to thank my wife, Wendy, for her patience and encouragement during the writing of this book. She kept the coffee flowing and confiscated my games disks – essential interventions for which I am truly grateful. I would also like to thank Christopher Riches at HarperCollins for his flexible interpretation of the word deadline.

Matthew Wall
May 2001

Contents

Chapter 1   Introduction   1

Chapter 2   Research Resources   7

Chapter 3   Schools and the National
                 Curriculum   41

Chapter 4   Teaching Resources for
                 Parents, Teachers and Pupils   51

Chapter 5   Further Education   69

Chapter 6   Safety Online   87

Chapter 7   Buying Online   109

Index   131

Introduction

Welcome to the *Sunday Times Guide to Education Online* – a jargon-free book designed to help you get the most out of the internet as a cornucopia of educational resources. This guide assumes that you are already familiar with the web and how to surf. If you're not, you may want to consider reading *The Sunday Times Guide to the Internet* first.

It is fitting that education is making a comeback online given that the internet was largely invented by academics wishing to create a more efficient way of sharing ideas and research. The internet has changed beyond all recognition since those early days, but the principles that underpinned its invention still hold true. The internet is a supremely efficient way of sharing information, and that is what makes it an excellent learning and educational tool. Not only that, but the web has now evolved into a rich, multimedia environment incorporating text, sound, video and animation. This is enabling learning resources to become much more interactive, providing a two-way, stimulating experience for children and adults alike.

As technology improves and internet access speeds increase with the introduction of large bandwidth connections,

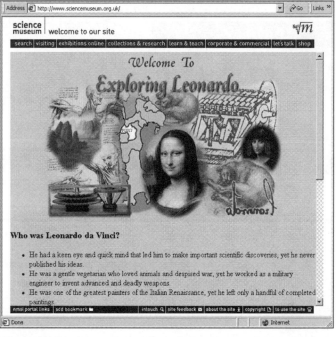

The internet has become an excellent educational tool, with its interactive, multimedia environment.

the quality of this interactivity will improve remarkably. For example, using standard 56kbps modems streaming video images are still very jerky and a far remove from television. Broadband connections will enable much more data to be transferred creating a smoother, more realistic picture. The pages of books, traditionally passive media, will come to life, enhancing the study of science and nature, for example. Dry concepts can be made more vivid using video and animation, and learning can be richer and more fun.

That's the theory at least, and I am an optimist when it comes to the internet's potential in the field of education. There are several pitfalls, however. The internet is the flavour of the month in educational and governmental circles. If you swallowed all the hype you could be forgiven for thinking that the web will turn us into a nation of geniuses overnight. As long as every schoolchild is online we will have reached educational nirvana it seems. The internet is still in its infancy and we're still a little starry-eyed about it. But we shouldn't forget that it is just a tool – a potentially powerful and important one, but a tool nonetheless. A tool – however excellent – doesn't make a skilled craftsman. Similarly, the internet, without the skills required to use it effectively, is a pretty blunt instrument, and a potentially dangerous one at that.

Firstly, it has been well documented how easily pornography and antisocial material can be accessed on the web. Even innocently chosen words entered into a search engine can throw up shocking results from time to time. Any parent or teacher wanting children to make the most of the web will need to take this into consideration. There are a number of security measures you can take, including the use of content-filtering software, but the only really reliable method is complete supervision (for more on security, *see* **Safety Online**, *page 87*).

Filtering software such as Cybersitter (www.cybersitter.com) can help to prevent unsuitable web content reaching young eyes.

3

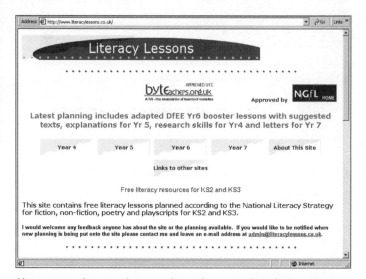

Using approved sites, such as www.literacylessons.co.uk, is the best way to ensure education on the web is accurate and worthwhile.

Secondly, there is just so much information on the web – around two billion web pages at the last count – and it is so easy to publish it there that sifting the wheat from the chaff is problematic. Learning to use search engines and directories is important, but so is learning how to spot stuff that is worth reading and stuff that isn't. Anyone can publish their opinions and advice on the web, but just how informed and credible such views are is often difficult to establish.

So in education, probably more than any other sphere, it is essential that websites are known to be authentic, well-researched and vetted. This isn't impossible. After all, it's the same with books. Students are given reading lists of approved texts and the same can be done for websites. It is when students are trying to find new sources of information themselves that the issue of credibility and factual accuracy arises. As a general rule, if there is no way of verifying online content from another source, it should be treated with

The internet is both an immense repository of knowledge and a valuable learning tool.

extreme caution. It is still true to say that on a large number of sites the standards of research are far from rigorous.

This issue has been particularly relevant to health information sites, where some unqualified 'practitioners' have been publishing unproven cures for cancer and other serious ailments. A well-designed website can give the patina of respectability to lure the desperate and unsuspecting. So the moral of the story is: stick to well-known, respected sites if you can, and try to verify new information from other sources as well.

What does this book cover?

Education online covers a wide range of topics, but there are two major themes: the web purely as a source of research and information, and the web as an interactive learning tool. There are many useful research tools online

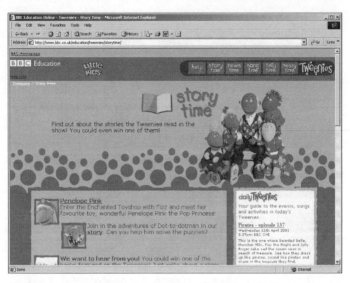

The internet has excellent educational sites for children of all ages.

these days, from encyclopaedias to thesauruses. A noticeable trend is the rise of online colleges and universities. Educational institutions can run courses remotely, allowing overseas students and others to take part. The increasing interactivity of the web is enabling online learning tools to become virtual lecture theatres. In a couple of years students could be having one-to-one tutorials over the web thanks to webcams and broadband high-speed connections.

The web is presenting educational opportunities to all age-groups, from tiny tots to silver surfers. For youngsters, there are plenty of educational games and pre-school learning sites where they can familiarise themselves with computers and keyboards in a fun environment. This book also looks at resources for parents and teachers, too, since the web can be a useful lesson planner and homework aid.

Perhaps most importantly of all, this guide tells you how to make the most of the web in safety and security – one of parents' main concerns when it comes to the internet.

Research Resources

Introduction

Imparting information is one of the things the internet does best. There is a wealth of research resources online these days, from encyclopaedias and dictionaries, to libraries and museums, from live news channels and newspapers, to academic journals and newsletters. The main problem is learning how to manage all these resources.

There are two main ways of finding what you want on the web. The first is to go direct to useful websites by typing in their web address in your browser address box. In this chapter we give you a range of useful addresses to get you started on your educational odyssey. Plus we show you how to save the addresses in your 'Bookmarks' or 'Favorites' folder so that you can revisit them easily without having to type out the addresses each time.

> **TIP**
>
> *If you do subscribe to mailing lists, save the e-mail that tells you how to unsubscribe, otherwise you may find your in-box filling up even after several attempts at stopping your subscription.*

The next method is to search the entire web using search engines and directories. We give you lots of examples, show you how to use them, and point out some of the pitfalls.

You can also have news and research delivered to you via e-mail newsletters. There are plenty of specialist online magazines and newspapers that allow you to sign up for their e-mail delivery services. You simply join the mailing list, pre-selecting the types of story or research you're interested in, then receive regular updates.

Finally, an informal, but nevertheless potentially invaluable, source of information and opinions is other people. Usenet is a part of the internet dedicated to discussion groups, or newsgroups as they're sometimes called. There are thousands of them, grouped by subject (for more on what they are and how to use them, *see* **Using newsgroups**, *page 16*).

One of the most widely used search engines: Excite (www.excite.co.uk).

Using search engines and directories

Using search engines and directories

With around two billion web pages on the internet these days, and hundreds more being added every day, the volume of information online can be overwhelming. We need help finding what we want, and that's where search engines, directories, databases and news resources come in.

A search *engine* searches all the web pages it can find, whereas a *directory* is simply an archived list of web pages, grouped according to subject category. What you tend to find is that the two words are used to mean the same thing even though they are different. As the internet mushrooms in size, the general trend is towards directories.

In theory, a search engine will therefore provide you with a more comprehensive search and a greater choice of results to look at. But this means a lot more work sifting through these results. Directories are an attempt to make the internet more manageable by listing those pages that editors think the surfing public will find most useful. Lack of thoroughness is the only disadvantage of this approach, although directories do serve most needs.

The good news is that search engines are becoming more sophisticated and better at pinpointing what you really want. Some engines, called meta-engines in the jargon, interrogate lots of other engines at the same time, making for an extremely thorough, if lengthy, search process.

> **TIP**
>
> Some engines, called meta-engines in the jargon, interrogate lots of other engines at the same time, making for an extremely thorough, if lengthy, search process.

So when carrying out online research for teaching or learning purposes, it is important to use a variety of search resources, as you are unlikely to find everything you want in one go. Don't assume that you can find everything online either. Content is only there because someone has bothered to put it there. It would take a gargantuan effort to put the entire contents of the British Library on the web, for example. The internet is still in its infancy and old-fashioned libraries are not dead yet, by any means.

How to search

Most search engines and directories follow a similar format – they have a search box where you enter in key words or phrases, you click on 'go' or 'search' or the equivalent word, and away you go. But unless you want to be inundated with irrelevant results that take an age to wade through, it pays to learn how to search 'intelligently'.

Much of the frustration associated with the use of search engines is caused by a lack of understanding about how to search. This isn't surprising as the rules are often very complicated and differ from site to site. But if you want to make the most of the web as a

> **TIP**
>
> *If you want to make the most of the web as a research tool, take the time familiarise yourself with a few basic search skills.*

research tool, take the time to familiarise yourself with a few basic search skills.

So-called Boolean logic, named after British mathematician George Boole, underpins most search engines. Words such as AND, OR and NOT, whether spelled out or assumed, help computers sift vast amounts of data. These words are called Boolean operators.

For example, if you typed in 'frog AND toad' the search engine would find all documents where both those words were mentioned. If you wrote 'frog OR toad', the search engine would have found all documents containing at least one of the words or both. This would have resulted in a much larger, and probably unmanageable, number of documents. Searching on 'frog NOT toad' would have thrown up documents containing the word frog but not the word toad. That's Boolean logic. Other useful words include NEAR, which ensures that the words you've chosen are in close proximity and not scattered at opposite ends of document with no relevance to each other at all.

You can also search for documents that contain derivations of words. For example, searching on medic* would give you documents containing all words beginning with 'medic', such as medication, medical, medicament and so on. This is useful if you want to take a broad-brush approach to a subject.

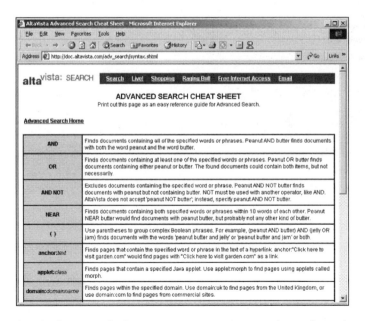

Learning how to use Boolean operators can save you many hours of wasted time on the net.

Brackets round search words like this: (search phrase) can also tell the engine that you want to search for the phrase within the brackets exactly as written, rather than each of the component words. Again, each engine will have its own version of this, so read up on the rules. In quite a few engines speech marks – "search phrase" – will do the same thing.

These days many search engines use their own versions of Boolean searching, assuming you want all your search words to be found, rather than just any, and vice versa with others. To confuse things further, some search engines use Boolean logic but denoted by different symbols. For example + and – before words can equate with AND and NOT. The treatment of upper and lower case can also be quirky.

It really is worth the effort finding out in detail the search system that a search engine or directory uses by investigating the 'Search Tips' section, usually found near the search box, or by choosing the 'Advanced Search' option. It may be frustrating to have to do this, but it will save you time in the long run.

To sum up, here are some general tips to make your searches more accurate and meaningful:

1 Try to use unique words and phrases.

2 Make sure you spell the words correctly.

> **TIP**
>
> *When you're browsing all the 'hits' thrown up by a search, open new browser windows when choosing the results you're most interested in. You can do this by clicking the right mouse button then choosing 'Open in New Window'. This means you can refer back to the search page more easily and look at several websites at once. It saves a lot of time.*

③ Use several words rather than just a couple to help narrow the field down.

④ Learn how different search engines handle upper and lower case.

⑤ Use Boolean operators where relevant (or the search engine's own version).

⑥ Compare results from several search engines or use a meta-search engine.

⑦ Try other sources of information within search engines, such as Usenet newsgroups, as well as the web.

The best search engines

If you are carrying out detailed academic research, then you need a really comprehensive engine or specialist directory relevant to the work you are doing. An engine like **Copernic** (www.copernic.com) will trawl through lots of other search engines, directories, Usenet lists (*see page 16*) and e-mail databases looking for what you want.

You need to download its browser software, which is closely integrated into the Microsoft Internet Explorer web browser, but once you've done this you have an excellent search tool on your desktop, capable of saving and categorising your searches. Of course, searching such a large number of other engines does take longer, but it is usually worth it.

TIP

If you are carrying out detailed academic research, then you need a really comprehensive engine or specialist directory relevant to the work you are doing.

A search engine called **Google** (www.google.com) is rightfully praised for the lightning speed of its searches. Just type a word or phrase, hit 'Return', and pages of relevant results pop up in typically half a second. It searches approaching 1.5 billion web pages. Well-known US search engines like AltaVista, Excite and Yahoo! have now introduced UK-specific sites. This helps reduce the number of irrelevant pages when searching.

A review site called **Search Engine Watch** (www.search enginewatch.com) looks at all the latest developments in search engines and gives more tips on how to conduct accurate searches.

Below is a list of the leading search engines, directories and other online research resources. You probably won't get round to using them all, but try several to see which ones you find the easiest to use and which provide the most useful and accurate search results.

The simpler the better – by not having any content of its own the Google search engine is fast, accurate and easy to use (www.google.com).

Search engines

AltaVista UK	www.uk.altavista.com
Excite UK	www.excite.co.uk
FastSearch	www.alltheweb.com
Go	www.go.com
Google	www.google.com
Goto	www.goto.com
HotBot	hotbot.lycos.com
Lycos	www.lycos.co.uk
Mirago	www.mirago.co.uk
NBCi	www.nbci.com
Northern Light	www.northernlight.com
WebCrawler	webcrawler.com

Search directories

Britannica	www.britannica.com
Yahoo!	www.yahoo.com
Yahoo! UK	uk.yahoo.com
About.com	www.about.com
DMOZ Open Directory Project	dmoz.org
The Argus Clearinghouse	www.clearinghouse.internet
Galaxy	www.galaxy.com
Magellan	magellan.excite.com
EuroSeek	www.euroseek.com
LookSmart	www.looksmart.com
UKOnline	www.ukonline.com
What's Online	www.whatsonline.co.uk
UK Plus	www.ukplus.co.uk
Search UK	www.searchuk.com
UK Max	www.ukmax.com

Meta-search engines

All4One	www.all4one.com
Copernic	www.copernic.com
MetaCrawler	metacrawler.com
Dogpile	www.dogpile.com
ProFusion	www.profusion.com
All-In-One	www.allonesearch.com
Ask Jeeves	www.ask.co.uk
Powersearch	www.powersearch.com

Using newsgroups (Usenet)

Usenet is the collective name for all the discussion groups and newsgroups. It is a dedicated section of the internet and as such, the newgroups have a different style of address. The **www** bit of the typical web address is replaced instead by an abbreviation such as **alt.**, **misc.**, **news.** or **talk.**, followed by subject headings. The categorisation of these subjects can be quite loose, so be prepared to range across different topics when searching for something specific.

WARNING

Adults should consider vetting the newsgroups that children have access to.

When you download 'news' on the net, it doesn't mean news in the conventional sense, but the messages left by people. These messages are called 'articles', too, just to complicate matters. Also, Usenet shouldn't be confused with bulletin boards or chat rooms. Bulletin boards tend to be places where people can swap messages on particular websites, and chat rooms are 'real-time' environments where people can exchange instantaneous messages.

There are thousands of these newsgroups on Usenet. The discussions are free-ranging and sometimes quite tempestuous. Usenet is largely self-regulating, apart from the usual laws of libel and defamation covering all publishing media, so adults should consider vetting the newsgroups that children have access to. Caveats aside, there is a potential goldmine of useful information to be found here. And with the multimedia nature of the internet, messages can now include photographs, video, animation and sound, too.

There are two main ways of accessing Usenet. The first is to use your newsreader program included with the latest versions of web browsers. Instead of accessing the web, you go to your internet service provider's 'news server' – a computer that deals exclusively with Usenet. You can browse all the groups and carry out detailed subject searches this way, choosing to subscribe to any groups you find interesting. This is a good way of managing your Usenet usage because you can save the messages to read offline, for example. This helps to cut down your phone bill.

> **TIP**
>
> *Using your newsreader program is a good way of managing your Usenet usage because you can save the messages to read offline, for example. This helps to cut down your phone bill.*

But you can also access all these newsgroups through the web, by going to sites such as **Google Groups (groups.google.com)** – formerly called Deja.com. Google is in the process of sharpening up the categorisation of the messages to make the database easier to use, but it is already excellent for precise subject searches. One useful innovation includes a bar next to the newsgroup subject heading that gives you an indication as to how active the group is. There is little point posting messages to a group that very few people access as you're unlikely to receive a reply. As with ordinary search engines, you have to search intelligently to achieve useable results. For example, simply typing 'education' into the search box threw up 377,000 entries when I tried.

You can either enter a more specific search term or browse the newsgroup subject titles looking for relevant groups. Here's a brief list of education-related newsgroups to get you started:

    alt.education.*
    alt.school.*
    humanities.*
    misc.education*
    sci.*
    soc.culture.*
    soc.history.*
    talk.philosophy.*
    talk.politics.*
    talk.religion.*
    talk.environment.*

Note: The asterisk indicates that there are various sub-groups within each category.

Tips on posting messages

Ongoing discussion topics are called 'threads' and you can simply reply to views already expressed or start a new thread if you like. People who post messages – 'posters' – may include their e-mail addresses so that you can contact them direct if you want. Don't give out your e-mail address as a matter of course though, or you might become the target of unwanted e-mails, known as 'spam'.

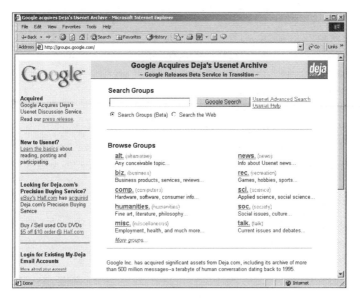

You can access newsgroups through websites such as Google.com (groups.google.com).

You can start a new message within your newsreader program by clicking on 'New Message' in the menu bar, or via a Usenet search engine, such as Google Groups mentioned above. To start a new message just click on the 'New Message' tabs in your newsreader menu bar.

WARNING

You can make yourself very unpopular if you waste people's time with irrelevant messages or annoying habits, such as typing in capitals – which is known as 'shouting'.

Before posting messages make sure you know a little about the Usenet etiquette. Read the Frequently Asked Questions (FAQ) file in the newsgroup if there is one, and look around for any other 'Help' files to get you started.

News resources

Nearly all the traditional media have realised that they cannot ignore the internet, even if they do perceive it to be a threat. Millions of us are still prepared to fork out for a daily paper and magazines and journals, yet the unwritten rule of the internet is that information is for free. If newspapers weren't so handy, portable and user-friendly, they probably would have dwindled rapidly already. As it is, talk of their imminent demise is greatly exaggerated. There are two main reasons for this. Firstly, only a quarter of the British adult population is online, and secondly, technology is still not sophisticated enough to make electronic newspapers a viable alternative for people on the move.

But although newspapers might not advertise their online presence very loudly, almost every national has a website containing most of the stories and features you would find in the paper itself. Sometimes the publishers try to differentiate the products by restricting some of the content to paying subscribers, or at least to people who register on the website. But by and large, online newspapers are a valuable free source of information. What's more, several of the papers offer truly comprehensive archive facilities, allowing you to look for stories in editions months or even years old. That's something the paper versions can't do very easily.

TIP

Several of the papers offer truly comprehensive archive facilities, allowing you to look for stories in editions months or even years old.

Luckily, the taxpayer-funded BBC doesn't have to worry too much about such commercial considerations and its website is a no-holds-barred, fully functional, interactive news paradise. It is definitely a site worth

The UK's most famous Sunday paper (www.sunday-times.co.uk) brings news from around the world direct to your desktop, together with in-depth comment and analysis on the issues that matter.

bookmarking (for how to do this, *see* **Saving website addresses for future reference**, *page 38*). Not only do you get written stories, but you can also see video footage and hear broadcasts via web radio, too.

Since high-speed internet connections are still not widespread it has to be said that live video and radio services are, as yet, far from perfect. A standard 56kbps modem isn't fast enough a lot of the time and video images can be extremely jerky, while radio broadcasts can break down altogether. Superior technology will rectify this, but we'll probably have to wait a couple of years before such high-speed 'broadband' connections become standard.

Keep up with the pace of political and economic change internationally with one of the world's most respected economic journals (www.economist.com).

It's easy to see why many think this is the best designed and most comprehensive news site around (news.bbc.co.uk). With up-to-the-minute news reporting, if it isn't on this site, it probably hasn't happened yet.

Below is a list of essential news resources.

National newspapers

The Sunday Times	www.sunday-times.co.uk
The Times	www.thetimes.co.uk
Financial Times	www.ft.com
Telegraph	www.telegraph.co.uk
Guardian	www.guardian.co.uk
Independent	www.independent.co.uk
Daily Mail	www.dailymail.co.uk
Mirror	www.mirror.co.uk
Express	www.express.co.uk
Evening Standard	www.thisislondon.co.uk

Specialist magazines and journals

Times Educational Supplement	www.tes.co.uk
Times Higher Educational Supplement	www.thes.co.uk
Times Literary Supplement	www.the-tls.co.uk
Primary Online	www.tesprimary.co.uk
The Economist	www.economist.com
The New Statesman	www.newstatesman.co.uk
The Spectator	www.spectator.co.uk
The New Scientist	www.newscientist.co.uk

News broadcasters

BBC	www.bbc.co.uk
ITN	www.itn.co.uk
PA Newswire	www.pa.press.internet
Reuters	www.reuters.com
CNN	www.cnn.com

News aggregators

BBC Monitoring (world news)	www.monitor.bbc.co.uk
NewsNow	www.newsnow.co.uk
Newswatch-UK	www.newswatch.co.uk
NewsHub	www.newshub.com

Technology News

Wired	**www.wired.com**
Internet.com	**www.internet.com**
Net Imperative	**www.netimperative.co.uk**
NUA Surveys	**www.nua.ie**

Government information

The government aims to deliver all public services online by 2005 in a £1 billion push to get the UK online. Part of this drive has involved the improvement in many government department websites. Until recently, online government consisted of a motley collection of

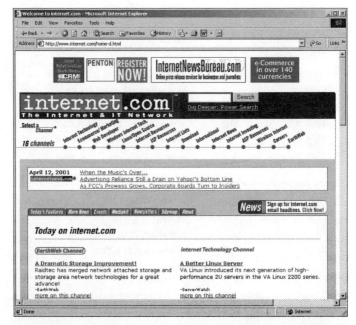

Written by people who really know their way around cyberspace, this site (www.internet.com) has news and views on all aspects of web technology.

badly designed sites operating a scatter-gun approach to the dissemination of information. There was little tailoring of data to meet specific needs and almost no interactivity. Thankfully the approach is now much more focused. Government departments are attempting to package the vast amounts of valuable data they hold for public consumption, as well as set up specific websites to promote certain government policies.

Here we list a few of the main gateway websites that should give you access to the major sources of official facts and figures, policy announcements and historical documents.

National Grid for Learning (www.ngfl.gov.uk)
The Grid is Tony Blair's ambitious plan to bring all aspects of education, whether formal or informal, academic or corporate, under one roof. He's hoping that learners, the education and lifelong learning services, and industry can all contribute to the development of the Grid.

Organisations and companies that want their content on the Grid have to go through a registration and approval process, which includes agreeing to be bound by the NGfL's code of conduct. The laudable idea is that the NGfL logo will give people confidence that they are visiting a site that has high quality standards. According to the website it now offers more than 5,000 pages of content hosted by other sites and 300,000 pages of indexed content. There are specific sites for Scotland, Wales and Northern Ireland, too, as well as for other UK regions. The aim is for the Grid, maintained by the British Educational Communications and Technology Agency (Becta), eventually to cater for the needs of everyone who wants or needs to learn. It doesn't yet, but it could with a decent following wind.

Open Gov (www.open.gov.uk)

This is the main government directory, listing all departments with links through to their websites. It is a straightforward, functional site designed and maintained by the Central Computer and Telecommunications Agency (CCTA), now part of the Office of Government Commerce.

Office of the E-Envoy (www.e-envoy.gov.uk)

The government set up a new post of 'e-envoy' in 2000 to oversee the 'UK Online' project. This is a good place to find out the latest news about moves to improve public sector online services.

UK Online (www.ukonline.gov.uk)

This is a new 'citizen information portal' that attempts to make public services more accessible and responsive to people's needs. Content has been specifically tailored around life events, such as having a baby, going away, dealing with crime, learning to drive, moving home, and death and bereavement. New topics will be added regularly and the aim is to incorporate interactive services, such as the ability to register the birth of a baby online. There's a section designed to encourage people to take a more active part in politics, too. You can register to participate in the consultation process, for example, and have your say on such scintillating topics as the 'licensing hours for New Year's Eve 2001 and during Her Majesty's Golden Jubilee in June 2002'. At least they're trying!

10 Downing Street (www.pm.gov.uk)

The Prime Minister has been leading by example with his well-designed site. It has colourful graphics, multimedia content and interactive elements built in. For example, there's a section called '10 out of 10' specifically for children. They can read about the history of No. 10 and put questions to ministers who take it in turn to be interviewed. Kids can also

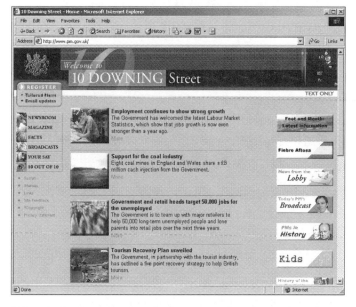

Full marks for this innovative and interactive site from the corridors of power (www.pm.gov.uk). The PM throws open the doors of his famous residence and the '10 out of 10' page encourages children to get involved in politics from an early age.

say what they would do if they were prime minister. Teachers are invited to provide feedback on the educational content of the site. The PM's efforts are certainly superior to many commercial websites.

The Public Record Office (www.pro.gov.uk)

The Public Record Office looks after all the national archives and has now redesigned its website to make it easier for researchers of all ages to use. It offers over eight million document references with plenty of links to other useful research sites, such as the Royal Commission on Historical Manuscripts. There's also a 'Virtual Museum' where you can find out more about the PRO and its 11th-century origins, and a site dedicated to helping you research family trees. An

'Education' section includes an award-winning resource called 'Learning Curve', which provides lessons and activities for Key Stages two to four. These can be used interactively or printed out for classroom use. All the Learning Curve exhibitions are designed to complement the National Curriculum History Study Units. The PRO site is a wonderful example of how good design and a more service-orientated approach can transform a government site into a valuable interactive educational resource.

National Statistics (www.ons.gov.uk)

For drier facts about births, marriages and deaths, population figures, and social surveys, the revamped National Statistics site is the place to go. It's not as user-friendly as it could be, but it's moving in the right direction.

OFSTED – Office for Standards in Education (www.ofsted.gov.uk)

OFSTED may be the bane of most teachers' lives, but its site is pretty useful for parents. You can find out how OFSTED's school inspection system works and read the reports for the majority of English schools in Adobe Acrobat format.

Online encyclopaedias, dictionaries and thesauruses

In the days when the *Complete Oxford English Dictionary* can fit on one or two CD-ROMs – with all the space and cost savings that entails – it is clear that the internet is a perfect medium for reference material. Cataloguing and cross-referencing have been revolutionised by increasingly powerful computers. There's so much reference material out there – hundreds of general-knowledge and subject-specific encyclopaedias are now online – that the sheer weight of it all can be overwhelming at first.

The only real danger you have to be on your guard against is the potential cultural bias of publishers. For example, when Microsoft's *Encarta* encyclopaedia first hit our shores it was quite clearly US-orientated with many UK-specific details omitted. The same obviously goes for dictionaries and thesauruses.

Rather than give individual web addresses for specific encyclopaedias and so on, we've collated some excellent directory sites that list as many reference sources as you could possibly need. You can then scroll through each of their lists to find exactly what you want, bookmarking your favourite sites for future use.

BUBL Information Service (www.bubl.ac.uk)
BUBL is a catalogue of 12,000 selected internet resources covering most academic areas of interest. Search on the word 'reference' and you get a list of 74 reference works with

Forget all those weighty encyclopaedic tomes putting your bookshelf out of shape. Here's the modern version — well-researched, updated continually and refreshingly advert-free, www.britannica.com is one of the fastest reference sites on the web.

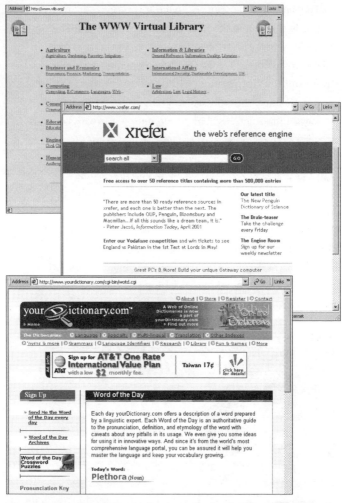

If you're trying to track down reference works, here's a few places from which to start: www.vlib.org (top), a virtual library created by Tim Berners-Lee, co-inventor of the web; www.xrefer.com (centre), a search engine that searches more than 50 major reference works including encyclopaedias, dictionaries, thesauruses and quotations; and www.yourdictionary.com (bottom), the largest collection of dictionaries on the web — more than 1,500 of them in a total of 230 languages.

accompanying descriptions, including popular favourites such as the **Encyclopaedia Britannica** (www.britannica.com). It is funded by the Joint Information Systems Committee of the Higher Education Funding Councils of England, Scotland and Wales and the Department of Education for Northern Ireland. As such it is very fast because it isn't bogged down by annoying graphics and banner adverts – a breath of fresh air in this commercial world.

The 3W Virtual Library (www.vlib.org)

This is a truly comprehensive directory of resources, founded by Tim Berners-Lee, the British co-inventor of the web. It is maintained by cohorts of academically-minded volunteers. Just click on the 'General Reference' section for encyclopaedias, libraries, dictionaries, lexicons, and glossaries galore. There are brief descriptions of the works, including the country of origin.

Xrefer (www.xrefer.com)

This is a search engine specifically for reference works, including dictionaries of quotations. It trawls through more than 50 reference titles containing 500,000-plus entries looking for your search terms.

yourDictionary.com (www.yourdictionary.com)

yourDictionary.com has collated some 1,500 dictionaries representing over 230 languages – the largest collection on the web. You can receive definitions in multiple languages and easily translate words into foreign languages. The site makes much of its academic rigour, steered as it is by an august panel of linguistic experts. Definitely one to bookmark.

Museums, libraries and art galleries

The British Museum (www.thebritishmuseum.ac.uk)

The British Museum website has recently been revamped to coincide with the unveiling of the museum's splendid new glass roof. The site has clearer navigation and brighter colours. Information about the collections is organised geographically – just click on the area of the world you want to explore and go through to a page telling you what the museum has. But don't assume that the collections are viewable online – there are just too many items to put on the website. You can find out about current and forthcoming exhibitions, how to get to the museum, and even what's on the menu in the restaurant.

The museum's Education Department is also in the process of extending its online resources. At the moment the site simply provides information on how to obtain educational material, web links and suggestions for further reading. Pharaoh fans can also go to the museum's dedicated

Navigate your way round the cultural world with ease on the British Museum's site (www.thebritishmuseum.ac.uk).

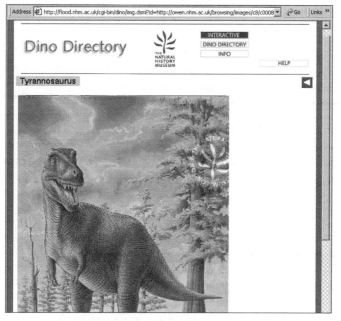

Address http://flood.nhm.ac.uk/cgi-bin/dino/img.dsml?id=http://owen.nhm.ac.uk/browsing/images/c8/c0008 ▼ | Go | Links »

Dino Directory

THE
NATURAL
HISTORY
MUSEUM

INTERACTIVE
DINO DIRECTORY
INFO

HELP

Tyrannosaurus

The Natural History Museum's fascinating site (www.nhm.ac.uk) seems to become more exciting every time you look at it and now has a huge range of resources for children and adults alike. Dinophiles will love the innovative 'Dino Directory' for all prehistoric creatures great and small.

Ancient Egypt site (www.ancientegypt.co.uk) – an excellent, well-illustrated and interactive education resource for parents, teacher and pupils alike. We can expect more of these subject-specific sites in future.

The Natural History Museum (www.nhm.ac.uk)
As well as the usual information about exhibitions, admission prices, and so on, the museum's education section has a range of resources for families, schools and adults wanting to learn more. For example, there are 28 'data files' on the dinosaurs with ideas on how they can be used at the museum. There are also interactive science experiments that schoolchildren can take part in.

The Science Museum (www.sciencemuseum.org.uk)

The Science Museum is actually part of the **National Museum of Science and Industry** (www.nmsi.ac.uk), which also incorporates the National Museum of Photography, Film & Television, and the National Railway Museum. Anyway, the Science Museum tells you about current exhibitions it is staging but also hosts several online exhibitions. It has laudably adapted its 'bricks-and-mortar' material for online consumption, including explanatory text, enlargeable pictures, and sound files. Some of these online learning resources it quaintly calls 'Exhiblets', meaning mini digital exhibitions. There's also a section specifically aimed at providing learning resources for teachers and pupils. In its efforts to make online learning a truly rewarding and interactive experience, the Science Museum is setting the pace that other museums will surely have to follow.

The Science Museum (www.sciencemuseum.org.uk) hosts a site full of discoveries waiting to happen. Its 'Exhiblets' section (mini digital exhibitions) houses some interesting learning resources.

Everything you'd expect from one of the largest information resources in the world (www.bl.uk), including access to over 18 million bibliographic records and a user-friendly document supply service.

The British Library (www.bl.uk)

The newly revamped British Library website includes a number of valuable online research tools for all shades of researcher. For example, Blaise – the British Library's Automated Information Service – provides access to 21 databases containing over 18 million bibliographic records. You have to pay for this, though. Simpler searches and document ordering can be carried out online, too, via the library's public catalogue. There's also plenty of well-illustrated information about current and forthcoming exhibitions.

3W Virtual Library Museums (vlmp.museophile.com)

This section of the Virtual Library contains a list of all the museums in the whole world, including the UK, with links through to their websites. Ones that have been particularly commended by users are given a special icon. Similarly, the art galleries section (vlmp.museophile.com/galleries.html) contains links to all the world's major galleries. It's all you need.

Miscellaneous research resources

● ●

BUBL Information Service (www.bubl.ac.uk/uk)

This site, mentioned above, also contains a useful directory of UK organisations and institutions, from charities to churches, football clubs to banks and building societies. Other sections include one dedicated to academic journals. It lists contents, abstracts or full texts of more than 200 journals and newsletters, with new titles being added on a regular basis.

Ingenta (www.ingenta.com)

This premier academic journal search engine lists around 1.4 million articles from 3,000 journals worldwide. Some are free, others you have to pay for. You can do so online using a credit card over a secure, encrypted link. Payment isn't debited from your account until the article arrives at your address.

Welcome to Scoot (www.scoot.co.uk) – the online business directory that will put an end to all those old Yellow Pages directories piling up in your living room. Track down long-lost friends, too, with the people finder, containing more than 17 million residential contacts.

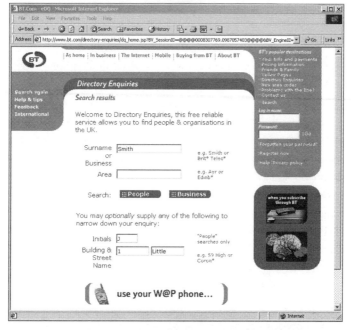

*Fed up with paying for the privilege of directory enquiries over the phone?
Then use the online service instead. The BT home page (www.bt.com)
contains a link to its directory enquiry service, to help you track down
that elusive name and number.*

Scoot (www.scoot.co.uk)

A comprehensive business directory with over two million
UK listings, Scoot also offers a people finder service, with
17 million residential phone numbers and addresses on
its database.

BT Directory Enquiries (www.bt.com/directory-enquiries/dq_home.jsp)

It is much cheaper to find out addresses and telephone
numbers online than to ring directory enquiries.
No wonder British Telecom doesn't choose to advertise
it too heavily. . .

Saving website addresses for future reference

Saving web addresses in your browser memory is an essential part of making the most of the internet and managing its vast information resources. This process is generally known as 'bookmarking', although Microsoft Internet Explorer calls bookmarks 'favorites' instead. The main advantage of bookmarking is that it saves you having to type out web addresses each time. Instead, you simply open your 'Bookmarks' (Netscape Navigator) or 'Favorites' (Internet Explorer) folder, click on the website you want to visit, and if you are not online already, you'll be connected to the internet and go straight to that website.

To bookmark pages in Netscape Navigator, go to the desired web page then click on the 'Bookmarks' pull-down menu and click the 'Add Bookmark' option. With Microsoft's Internet Explorer you click on the 'Favorites' pull-down menu and then click on 'Add To Favorites'. You can also click on the right mouse button while pointing at the page and you'll be offered the same options. Or, in Windows, you can just hold down the 'Control' button and press 'D' on your keyboard and it will bookmark the page in both browsers.

TIP

Organising your bookmarks into easily identifiable folders is a good idea if you want to use the web efficiently.

You can also tell your browser to store all the pages on your computer's hard drive so that you can view them again without having to go online. This is a useful feature that can help cut down your telephone bill. Of course, it is best suited to sites whose information isn't likely to change very often, otherwise you may end up reading stuff that is out of date. To prevent this happening you can also tell your browser to check for updated versions of the saved pages

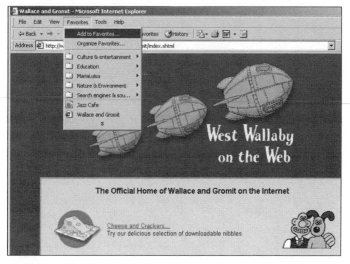

Bookmark your favourite websites in Internet Explorer to revisit them easily whenever you wish. Here it's www.aardman.co.uk.

next time you go online. You can then save the new pages for offline viewing later.

Organising your bookmarks into easily identifiable folders is a good idea if you want to use the web efficiently. In Internet Explorer you choose 'Organize Favorites' from the 'Favorites' menu. In Netscape Navigator you can choose 'Communicator', 'Bookmarks', 'Edit Bookmarks', or, more

TIP

Hold down the 'Control' button and press 'D' on your keyboard and it will bookmark the page in both Internet Explorer and Netscape Navigator.

directly, click on the dedicated 'Bookmarks' tab and then choose 'Edit Bookmarks'. You can call your bookmarks anything you like.

Chapter 3

Schools and the National Curriculum

Introduction

In these days of school league tables and supposed parental choice, parents have more information at their fingertips than ever before. Boning up on the best nurseries, primary and secondary schools to send your little darlings to is easy thanks to the web. All the performance data you could wish for is at hand. Not only that, but parents can have a look at school websites, too, and get more of a feel for the quality and ethos of the institutions – not that this should replace a visit in person, of course.

As well as detailed information about schools, parents can also find lots about government education policy and get to grips with the requirements of the National Curriculum. There are also more parent help sites springing up designed to give and swap advice about all things educational, from revision techniques to help if a child is being bullied. *See* **Teaching Resources for Parents, Teachers and Pupils**, *page 51* for more information.

In short, parents are being empowered by the information they can easily glean from the internet. With luck, this will encourage greater involvement in education generally, give children more support, and make schools feel that all their efforts are not going unnoticed.

Below is a list of websites that will help you choose the right schools, understand the education system and the National Curriculum, and generally prepare for launch on the schooling highway.

Department for Education and Employment (DfEE) Parents' Gateway (www.dfee.gov.uk/parents)

You have to applaud the efforts civil servants are making to create more relevant and helpful websites. Government departments have reams of valuable data and information that they used to keep locked away, jealously guarded. Now they are opening up, packaging advice and public policy information in more accessible ways on a variety of targeted websites. The DfEE in particular has been very busy creating a number of new sites designed to appeal to specific audiences. Its Parents' Gateway has a number of relevant links, the best of which are summarised below.

In the **Parents' Centre (www.parents.dfee.gov.uk)** parents can find out exactly what is being taught in the classroom, how their children are tested, and all about admissions policies. The resources are very wide and deep, with information on everything from literacy and numeracy to special educational needs. You can even find out about school meals and check the address of your local education authority if you like. Soon the DfEE will include links through to all LEA websites as well. All aspects of school are covered here, including related social issues, such as bullying, drugs and truancy. It is a comprehensive resource that can only get better and better as more links are included and more interactive elements incorporated.

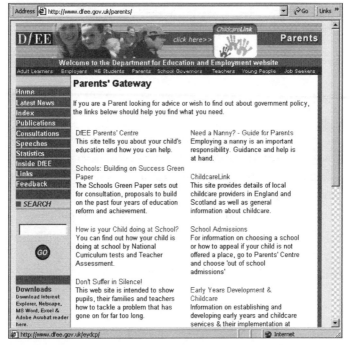

The Parents' Gateway (www.dfee.gov.uk/parents) is part of the DfEE's laudable attempt to make information on education more freely available to parents.

Complementing the 'In School' section is an 'Out of School' section, broadly covering all matters relating to children outside the alma mater. There is plenty of advice on choosing a school, explanations of admissions policies, what to do if your child is not accepted at the school of your choice, and so on. There are sections to help with learning at home – including advice on how to read with your children – revising and doing homework, with links to useful research resources, such as libraries, museums and galleries.

School Search (**www.parents.dfee.gov.uk/find/ multisearch.cfm**) allows you to carry out multiple searches, interrogating the DfEE School Performance Tables, School

Some of the most helpful sections of the Parents' Gateway are shown here. In the Parents' Centre (top, www.parents.dfee.gov.uk), you can find out how to get your child into a school, what they'll be taught when they get there and even what they'll have for lunch. Another section (centre, www.dfee.gov. uk/ncat) shows you exactly how and why testing in schools takes place. There is a very supportive section on bullying (bottom, www.dfee.gov.uk/ bullying), which advises parents and children on how to combat what is becoming a nationwide problem.

Website Database and OFSTED School Reports, for primary and secondary schools. It's all you need in one simple search engine – an excellent resource.

The Parents' Centre also includes other useful sections, such as recommendations for interesting days out, and 'Learning Journey', its guide to the National Curriculum. There's also education news, an online magazine for parents, and links to many other learning resources collated by the **National Grid for Learning (www.ngfl.go.uk).**

All about testing and teacher assessments (www.dfee.gov.uk/ncat) is the section of the Parents' Gateway that answers most of your questions about testing in schools – why and how it is done, and how teachers assess your child's performance.

Don't Suffer in Silence (www.dfee.gov.uk/bullying) addresses bullying, a big problem in some schools. Bullying can make children's lives a misery, and if not confronted, can lead to life-long emotional scarring and, rarely, child suicide. This section of the Parents' Gateway provides advice and other online resources to help children, teachers and parents combat the problem. The site is organised according to what your experience of bullying is, whether you're the victim, the parent or the teacher. For example, there's advice for families on how to spot child behaviour that may result from bullying. After all, you can't rely on a child to tell you what's happening – he or she may be ashamed, afraid, or both. There are links to anti-bullying websites, such as **Pupiline** (www.pupiline.net) and the **Anti-Bullying Network** (www.antibullying.net).

Need a Nanny? (www.dfee.gov.uk/nanny) caters for parents who need or want to work after having children and have the added pressure of sorting out childcare. The DfEE has produced a useful guide to employing a nanny and the responsibilities that entails. Similarly, its excellent

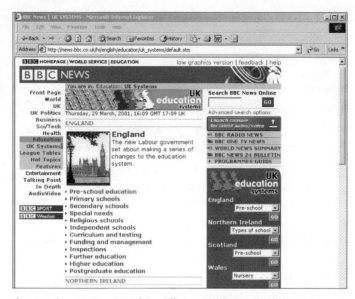

A comprehensive overview of the different education systems throughout the UK forms part of the BBC News website (news.bbc.co.uk).

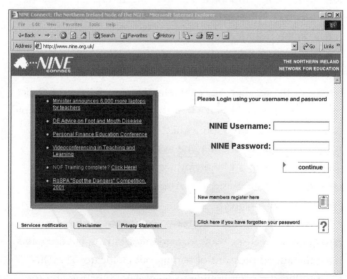

This simply designed site (www.nine.org.uk) advises on education in Northern Ireland as well as providing useful links to other educational sites.

ChildcareLink section (www.childcarelink.gov.uk) gives you help in finding a registered childminder, kids' club or nursery in your area.

Schoolsnet (www.schoolsnet.com)

This education portal (reviewed in greater depth later in the book – *see page 54*) features a fairly comprehensive schools guide providing information on over 22,000 schools, including 16,907 state primaries, 3,824 state secondaries, 455 preparatory schools, and 1,016 independent secondaries. At the time of writing the guide included just basic information about each school, but the aim is to add examination or key stage results, inspection reports, and fuller background details. This kind of information is already available for some schools, which are listed in bold type on the website.

BBC Guide to the UK's education systems (news.bbc.co. uk/hi/english/education/how_the_education_systems_work/ newsid_528000/528743.stm)

If you've always had a vague idea that 'they do things a bit differently in Scotland' when it comes to education, you might benefit from this overview of how the various systems differ in England, Wales, Scotland and Northern Ireland.

The Scottish Executive (www.scotland.gov.uk)

This umbrella site for devolved government in Scotland contains the latest news about education policies and links to other official Scottish sites.

Northern Ireland Network for Education (www.nine.org.uk)

As well as providing links to educational establishments in Northern Ireland, this site provides help for teachers, and pupils from the ages of five to 19.

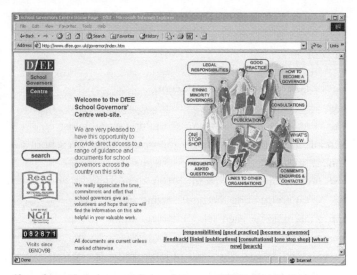

If you fancy playing a more direct role in your child's education, find out what it's like to become a school governor with the DfEE's handy guide (www.dfee.gov.uk/governor).

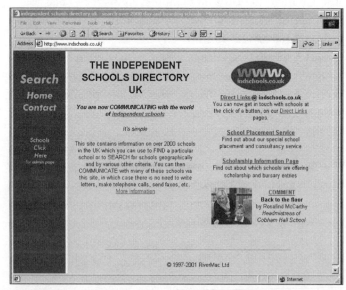

If you're thinking of educating your children privately, check out this portal (www.indschools.co.uk) for access to 2,000 independent schools in the UK.

Support for parents and children with special educational needs (www.becta.org.uk/inclusion/sen/orgs/links.html)
The British Educational Communications and Technology Agency has devoted a section of its site to special needs. There are lots of links to relevant organisations.

Becoming a school governor (www.dfee.gov.uk/governor/index.htm)
So you've looked at the performance tables, read the OFSTED report, pored over the school's website, and secured a place at the school for your child. How do you fancy becoming a governor? Get involved in the running of your child's school and really feel as if you're making a difference. This DfEE site gives you advice on how to become a governor and an overview of your responsibilities. Also have a look at **Govern Your School** (www.governyourschool.co.uk), a site created for and by school governors.

Going independent

The Independent Schools Directory (www.indschools.co.uk)
If you can't find what you're looking for in the state sector, there are always the fee-paying schools to consider. This useful portal site allows you to learn about and communicate with more than 2,000 UK independent day and boarding schools. You can also check which schools are offering scholarship and bursary entries.

Chapter 4

Teaching Resources for Parents, Teachers and Pupils

Introduction

There are plenty of online learning resources around for parents, teachers and pupils alike. Through the growing number of specialist education websites teachers can tap into a range of lesson ideas or chat to fellow professionals in virtual staffrooms. Increasingly, online purchasing of school equipment and books is being offered, too. Pupils can access a number of revision help websites, or simply visit sites of academic interest, either carrying out their own searches or going to sites recommended by teachers and other educationalists.

All these tools are there to be used, not as a replacement for traditional teaching and learning methods, but as a complement to them. There are websites that attempt to cater for all constituencies – parents, teachers and pupils – and some that are more specific. Below we give some of the best educational portal websites that provide excellent launch pads, plus a selection of more specialised sites. Inevitably, given that many of these sites include links to other related sites, there will be some overlap. But that's just the way the web is – a web!

Education portal sites

BBC Online Webguide (www.bbc.co.uk/webguide)
Just click on the 'Education' link of the BBC's awesomely comprehensive web guide and then bookmark that page immediately. There are links to hundreds of educational websites categorised according to subject and with information about the National Curriculum Key Stages that the sites cater for. A great starting point.

4Learning (www.4learning.co.uk)
Channel 4's education website is a well-laid-out effort organised intuitively according to the age group of the target audience. The online learning resources are closely linked to Channel 4's 400 hours of educational programming, including lesson ideas and interactive games and tests. There's also background material to the rest of its educationally relevant programming.

EduWeb (www.eduweb.co.uk)
EduWeb is an excellent resource for both teachers and pupils. It has several sections offering different services. For example, 'Pathways' is a database of more than 4,000 educational web pages searchable by age range, subject, or search phrase. The selected sites are rated by users through an online voting system that helps keep EduWeb on its toes and providing a relevant and high-quality service. There's also a large directory of school, college and Local Education Authority web pages where you can look at newsletters, examples of pupils' work, and the usual reports of school activities.

Two of the best education portal sites: the BBC online guide (top, www.bbc.co.uk/webguide) is the perfect gateway to hundreds of education sites and in-depth information about the National Curriculum, while Channel 4 has really done its homework to produce a well-organised, interactive site, with tie-ins to its educational television programmes (bottom, www.4learning.co.uk).

Teaching Resources

Plus, EduWeb provides schools and colleges with the facilities to create their own web pages in a protected environment through its 'Internet for Learning' subscription service. Teachers can link up to arrange inter-school projects or enter an online staffroom where they can share opinions, news and educational source materials. As if all this were not enough, there's also a 'Living Library', giving parents, teachers and pupils access to more than two million articles covering every subject in the National Curriculum.

Schoolsnet (www.schoolsnet.com)

This is another great all-round resource aimed at parents, teachers and pupils, providing tailored content to meet the needs of each constituency. One of the most impressive features is a fairly comprehensive schools guide providing information on more than 22,000 schools, including 16,907 state primaries, 3,824 state secondaries, 455 preparatory schools, and 1,016 independent secondaries. At the time of writing, the guide included only basic information about each school, but the aim is to add examination or Key Stage results, inspection reports, and fuller background details. This kind of information is already available for some schools, which are listed in bold type in the website.

Schoolsnet has also developed its own range of lesson ideas for teachers based on the various Key Stages of the National Curriculum. Pupils can receive help with their GCSE revision through Schoolsnet's growing number of revision modules. These include interactive animated graphics with self-test questionnaires that then tell you how much you scored. When I tried a few of them out I did spot a few gremlins, such as the odd question missing and a typing error here or there. But let's hope such mistakes are just teething problems. The concept is a good one and could benefit pupils.

Topmarks (www.topmarks.co.uk)

This is a very good directory of websites for teachers, parents and pupils. It includes more than 1,450 sites selected for their user-friendly design and relevance to National Curriculum subjects. Searching the database is easy since the sites are categorised according to subject. The reassuring point about Topmarks is that it has been going for several years already and has consistently picked up plaudits along the way. The authors have had time to refine and revise their service to make it as functional and accessible as possible. There is a separate section for parents that includes guides on literacy

Top marks indeed for this excellent directory of nearly 1,500 sites, searchable by subject (www.topmarks.co.uk). The sites have been chosen for their user-friendly design, making them ideal for teachers, parents and pupils.

and numeracy, and one for teachers with useful links to sites dedicated to supporting teachers and their interests and needs. Teachers can also take part in the Topmarks forum, swapping opinions and teaching tips on the site's bulletin board. Plus, there's a daily news service, collating the latest articles on general education topics. This is definitely a site to put at the top of your bookmarks list.

By Teachers (www.byteachers.org.uk)
Teachers, quite rightly, are a sceptical lot when it comes to supposedly wonderful new teaching methods and wheezes. They've seen them come, they've seen them quietly dropped – normally when a new government comes in. So, new-fangled websites claiming to be the Holy Grail of teaching are likely to be given a withering look. Teachers are more likely to trust websites produced by teachers themselves.

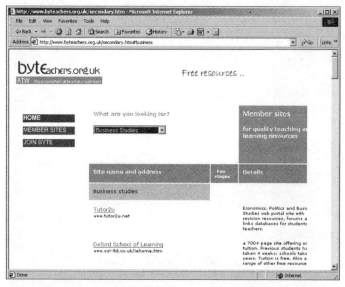

Here's education seen from the other side – by the teachers themselves. Byteachers.org.uk is a collection of more than 20 sites, written and approved by teachers, to promote quality teaching materials on the internet.

By Teachers was formed in March 2001 with such sceptical teachers in mind. It is a collection of educational websites that has formed an alliance called the Association of Teachers' Websites (ATW). Its aim is to promote awareness of just what is out there by way of free online teaching materials. It incorporates around 20 primary and secondary teaching websites.

Any website wanting to join the Association has to include high-quality teaching resources, be run by teachers, and be free to use. Perhaps crucially, new websites have to be approved by the other members of the Association before they can join. This kind of vetting by 'peer review' should ensure that high standards are maintained. The longer-term aim is to create a virtual school offering a range of interactive online lessons using the resources supplied by the member websites.

The two founders of the ATW, both ex-teachers, have their own subject-specific websites, one for English teachers called **teachit** (www.teachit.co.uk) and one dedicated to history called **Spartacus Educational** (www.spartacus.schoolnet. co.uk).

Early years websites

As research into child development continues to stress the importance of those pre-school and primary school years, a growing number of websites are springing up with help for parents on how to stimulate and entertain their children. Not only does the web offer lots of fun learning games online, it also helps familiarise young children with computers from an early age. There are scores of sites available – have a look at the Parents' Area section of the Topmarks website mentioned above for more than 80 suggestions. Below is just a selection of excellent resources for parents with tiny tots and primary school age kids.

DynaMo from BBC Education (www.bbc.co.uk/education/ dynamo/home.shtml)

This brightly coloured BBC Education site is aimed at children aged five to seven, with support ideas for parents. You'll find that quite a few of these early years websites feature cuddly cartoon characters, and DynaMo is no exception. I couldn't tell you what kind of animal DynaMo is supposed to be, but it is interested in learning. The site has a quiz and spelling games section (for which you need the Flash and Shockwave software readers, or plug-ins to use the jargon) and a history

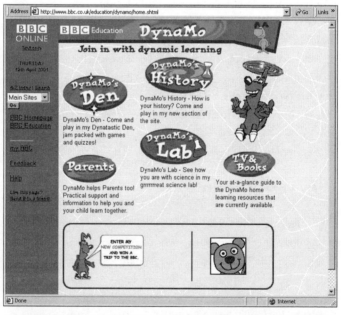

DynaMo is the star of this bright, friendly learning site from the BBC. It's aimed at five- to seven-year-olds, with plenty of advice for parents on how to help their children make the most of it (www.bbc.co.uk/education/ dynamo/home.shtml).

section, with interactive tests looking at the differences between Victorian and modern-day ways of living, for example. These Shockwave programs use Flash animation that does take a little while to load, so be patient, but it's worth it for the added fun of movement and sound. Kids can practise manipulating the mouse to make the most of the learning games. The fact that you can print off some of the exercises means that you don't have to be online all the time to make the most of the games. There's plenty of advice for parents on how to help their children through the site, and information on how the games conform to National Curriculum requirements.

Words and Pictures (www.bbc.co.uk/education/ wordsandpictures)
Another BBC Education site aimed at children aged five to seven that ties in with the television programme of the same name. This one concentrates on reading and writing, exploring the building blocks of words, from consonant clusters to long vowel sounds. The site is clearly laid out with many interactive features.

Little Animals Activity Centre (www.bbc.co.uk/education/ laac)
I make no apologies for featuring all these BBC Education websites. The truth is that they are very good, and the fact that the sites complement the television programmes – a large part of children's lives these days – makes them even more appealing. This site is aimed at four- to eight-year-olds and includes maths and spelling games, plus an activity centre featuring recipes and finger puppet templates for children to download and print off. The use of activity ideas that don't mean kids have to sit in front of a computer screen all the time is especially welcome. You can listen to stories or

Two wonderful websites guaranteed to invoke pleasure in children and nostalgia in adults: Ladybird (top, www.ladybird.co.uk) and Peter Rabbit (bottom, www.peterrabbit.com).

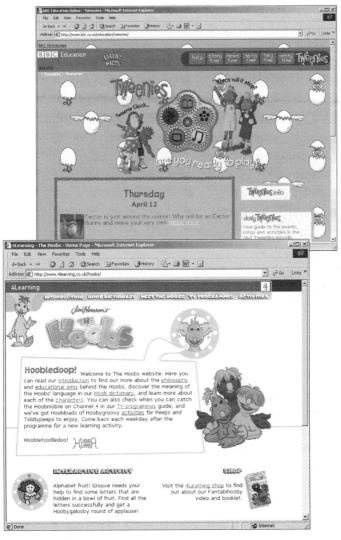

The BBC hosts the website of the hugely successful TV programme, the
Tweenies (top, www.bbc.co.uk/education/tweenies), aimed at those who've
outgrown the Teletubbies but who still want entertainment with their
education. Channel 4's answer to the Tweenies, the Hoobs (bottom,
www.4learning.co.uk/hoobs), travel through space and make discoveries on
the way.

read them online and play music games. The site makes full use of the internet's multimedia qualities and deserves a lot of credit.

Teletubbies (www.bbc.co.uk/education/teletubbies)
If you stay awake at night worrying about who spilled the Tubby custard, or you want to go counting giant rabbits with Laa-Laa, the Teletubbies site is a must. Although most parents have probably had enough of the 'eh-oh' cuddly aliens already, after a daily diet of the TV programme, the site does offer some fun interactive activities, such as colouring in online (no mess!). In fact, there are 120 online activities to choose from, including teaching toddlers the difference between left and right. Bill and Ben never did that.

The Tweenies (www.bbc.co.uk/education/tweenies)
Tiny tots weaned off the Teletubbies move on to the Tweenies as they get older, or so the BBC hierarchy would like us to think. The immense success of the programme seems to bear this out. Kids can find out more about all their favourite characters, listen to the latest pop single online, and review Tweenies books on the site. Not overly educational, but probably diverting for Tweenies fans.

The Hoobs (www.4learning.co.uk/hoobs)
Channel 4's attempt to compete with the BBC's Teletubbies and Tweenies phenomena is the Hoobs – more cuddly creatures for pre-school kids created by Muppet man Jim Henson. They are intergalactic travellers who do a lot of discovering along the way. As well as a daily programme, the website features a dictionary and encyclopaedia of the knowledge they have collected in transit. A word of warning: this is a world in which children are referred to as 'Tiddlypeeps' and the standard welcome is 'Hoobledoop! Hoobledoop! Whoop! Whoop! Whoop!'.

Ladybird (www.ladybird.co.uk)
A beautifully colourful animated site from the well-known children's book publisher. The eponymous insect features large in the site design, making it an instant hit with children. You can find out about the latest books in the series and play online games, such as 'Incy Wincy Spider' and 'Bears and Balloons'. And then you can let the kids have a go! Some of the stories are online and there are sections for parents and teachers, too, with advice on how to read with children and use the site effectively.

Fun With Spot (www.funwithspot.com)
Accept no imitations – this is the official Spot website based on the books by Eric Hill. Click on any of the brightly coloured objects in Spot's room and off you go on another adventure with the lovable scamp/annoying canine (delete as appropriate). The site is exactly like the books, but you can send postcards from it or print off the pictures for colouring in.

Peter Rabbit (www.peterrabbit.com)
More children's favourites with Beatrix Potter's traditional characters getting hip with it on the web. You can find out about the author's life and work and have fun with a few interactive sections, such as 'Tom Kitten's Playground' and 'Squirrel Nutkin's Film Show'.

There are some nice rustic sounds to add to the experience, but it has to be said that the site is mainly there to promote the various videos, CD-ROMs and books. It is well designed and pretty to look at though.

The British Association for Early Childhood Education (www.early-education.org.uk/parents.htm)
Plenty of advice and teaching ideas for parents with pre-school and older children. You can download documents in Rich Text Format.

Sites just for teachers

A lthough several of the educational portal sites mentioned above include sections aimed at teachers – featuring innovations such as virtual staffrooms, for example – there are a number of dedicated teacher-only sites. Here are some suggestions.

Virtual Teacher Centre (vtc.ngfl.gov.uk)
Part of the National Grid for Learning, the Virtual Teacher Centre provides a wealth of resources for teachers, including links to software providers and useful educational websites. Teachers can swap views in discussion forums and read up on the latest education news.

TeacherNet (www.teachernet.gov.uk)
Another site from the DfEE designed for teachers. It includes the usual links to useful websites and will soon incorporate more than 1,000 teacher-evaluated lesson plans and resources. Teachers can also gen up on career development issues and job vacancies – subjects always very close to teachers' hearts.

National Curriculum Online (www.nc.uk.net)
A DfEE site dedicated to explaining all aspects of the National Curriculum to schoolteachers. The government is trying to encourage teachers to submit their own favourite educational websites to build up a database of useful resources for other teachers. The most popular sites are shown first in searches. So far the database contains some 230 sites, searchable by subject. If teachers don't mind co-operating with the government, this site could become a valuable resource for teachers and parents alike.

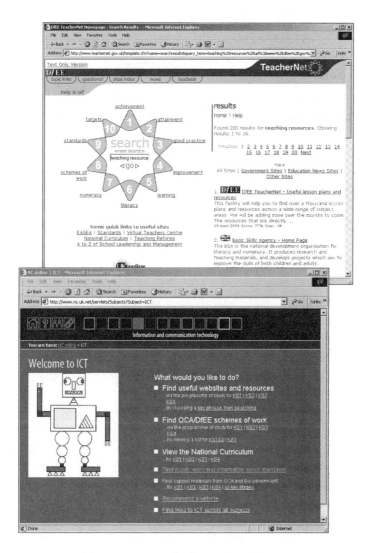

A couple of DfEE sites aimed specifically at teachers: TeacherNet (top, www.teachernet.gov.uk) provides teaching resources and career advice, while www.nc.uk.net (bottom) attempts to explain the National Curriculum and encourage teacher co-operation with the government.

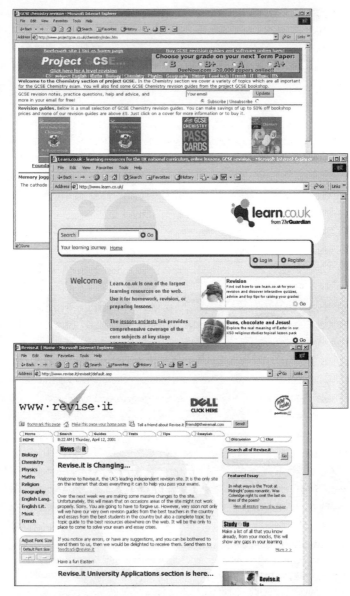

Most students hate revision, but here are some sites to help you revise effectively: www.projectgcse.co.uk (top), www.learn.co.uk (centre) and www.revise.it (bottom).

Revision help

The internet should never be thought of as a replacement for books, but it can be a useful supplement. There are several websites dedicated to helping angst-ridden teenagers cope with the trials of GCSEs and A-Levels as best they can.

BBC Education (www.bbc.co.uk/education/gcsebitesize)
The BBC's well-resourced and exhaustive education section covers most aspects of education. Its GCSE section is particularly good for maths and English revision. The chemistry and biology pages are good, too. The site includes revision and test facilities in a whole range of GCSE subjects, from maths to design technology. There's also an 'Ask the Teacher' facility that allows students to e-mail questions to a teacher. How soon they get a reply is another matter. For help with Scottish exam revision, go to the BBC's Scottish education site at **www.bbc.co.uk/scotland/revision**.

Sam Learning (www.samlearning.com)
A highly recommended revision site endorsed by the National Association of Head Teachers and the National Grid for Learning. It provides 28 online revision courses covering SATs, GCSEs and A-levels. There's software integration for use offline and at school.

GCSE Answers (www.gcse.com)
This site concentrates on Maths, English, Physics and French and includes exam papers, books and information about examining boards.

Project GCSE (www.projectgcse.co.uk)
A more comprehensive site featuring most GCSE subjects together with revision notes, test questions and advice on how to approach exams.

Learn (www.learn.co.uk)

This is a wonderful site from *The Guardian* newspaper, containing over 4,000 pages of curriculum material that can be used for learning and revision. There are test papers and lessons, plus a web guide full of links to educationally useful websites.

Revise It (www.reviseit.com)

Tips, tests and guides galore, plus advice for older children on how to apply successfully to college or university.

Chapter 5

Further Education

Introduction

This chapter looks at how school-leavers and mature students can use the internet to find out about further education and continuous learning. It also looks at some of the new online universities and colleges that are beginning to emerge and the development of distance learning in general.

There is no doubt that people in education acknowledge the great potential of the internet as an interactive learning tool. But there is also concern that it could be perceived as a cheap option for educational establishments and that face-to-face teaching, considered crucial by many, could be lost in this new digital world. Some worry that opportunists could set up online colleges in the hope of capitalising on this potentially global market,

WARNING

Make sure you take soundings about an institution's credentials and standing before committing to any online learning course.

without having the necessary pedigree to do so.

Anyone considering embarking on an online distance-learning course will have to take soundings about the institution's credentials and standing before committing to anything. There's little point studying hard to end up with a certificate that nobody respects.

Going to university or college

Deciding which college or university to go to can be tricky. Firstly, children and parents have to be realistic about whether the necessary grades can be achieved, and secondly, not all institutions will suit the personality of the student. At least the internet is providing a relatively easy way of finding out much more about such places – what they require and what they can offer.

Here are some useful websites to begin your research:

UCAS – Universities and Colleges Admissions Service (www.ucas.ac.uk)

UCAS is the UK central organisation that processes applications to full-time undergraduate courses, HNDs and university diplomas. This site is a must for anyone considering higher education. You can search for courses that may interest you, as well as by institution and you can even apply to become a student online. UCAS also provides links to all those colleges and universities with websites. A growing number of institutions have set up their own sites nowadays, but don't expect the same level of sophistication from each. They differ radically in quality and ease of use. A number of institutions give entry profiles detailing what qualifications you're likely to need to get a place.

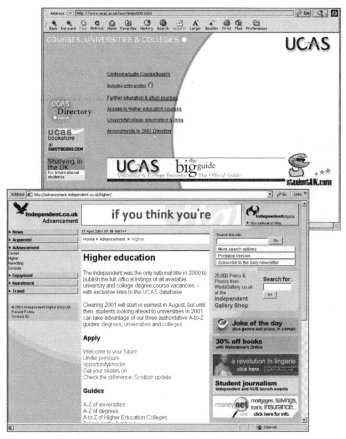

There are a number of useful websites to look at when deciding which college or university to go to. An invaluable undergraduate site (top, www.ucas.ac.uk) is run by UCAS, the institution that processes applications for university places. Another very handy guide to further education (bottom, advancement.independent.co.uk) is sited by the Independent.

The Independent Guides (advancement.independent. co.uk/higher)

Useful guides to degrees, universities and colleges are available from this respected broadsheet.

Study UK (www.studyuk.hobsons.com)

This site tells you all about studying in the UK and about UK universities and colleges. There's a useful section on the costs involved, such as accommodation and travel, as well as views from students.

The Student Loans Company (www.slc.co.uk)

These days being a student is not cheap and many leave college saddled with debt. But if you need money, you need money. Find out if you are eligible for a loan, what the terms are, and how to make an application.

Map of UK Universities (www.scit.wlv.ac.uk/ukinfo/ uk.map.html)

If getting as far away from your parents and annoying siblings is more important than the course you do, this site from the University of Wolverhampton might help. It shows exactly where all the universities are located.

Sites for students

Gradunet (www.gradunet.co.uk)

After you've finished loafing around for three years and real life is threatening to bite you on the backside, check out this virtual careers office and look for a job. The site includes career advice and help on writing a CV that won't be instantly binned.

StudentUK (www.studentUK.com)

An excellent portal site just for students, featuring all the usual sections, from chat rooms to entertainment guides, sex advice and how to get stuff on the cheap. Let's hope most students are too busy working or having a good time to spend too much time surfing the web.

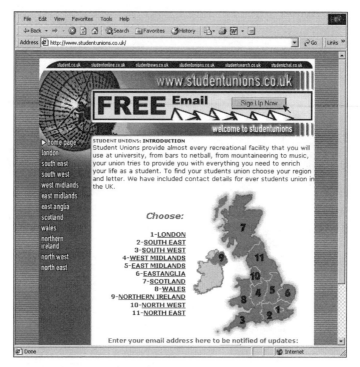

Ever wondered what your student union actually does? Then why not ask them? This site (www.studentunions.co.uk) lists every student union in the UK so you can contact them before you get there.

Higher Education Students' Gateway (www.dfee.gov.uk/ hestudents/index.shtml)

Part of the Department for Education and Employment, this site features several useful links for students, including advice on how to get funding, apply for post-graduate research places, and find employment in the real world.

> **TIP**
>
> *Also check out the newspapers and other media listed in Research Resources, page 7 as many of them offer dedicated student sections.*

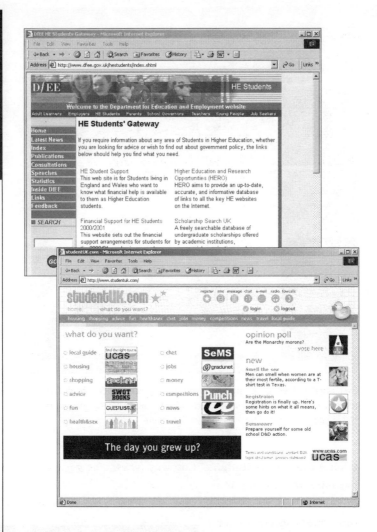

Student advice: the DfEE's directory for students (top, www.dfee.gov.uk/ hestudents/index.shtml) talks about all aspects of applying for university, as well as how to get a job when you finish, while the excellent portal site www.studentuk.com (bottom) offers a survival guide for students, from academic and social advice, to chat rooms and coping with disabilities.

Higher Education and Research Opportunities
(www.hero.ac.uk)

HERO is a comprehensive database of higher education and academic research links for the UK. It features sections tailored for people who work in higher education and for students.

Student Unions (www.studentsunion.co.uk)

An A–Z of student unions across the UK to stir those radical bones in you.

Distance learning

Distance learning has been around for a long time, fulfilling the needs of all those who may need extra qualifications for career advancement, or who left school without much to show for it. It is ideal for people who travel about a lot or who cannot or will not conform to institutional timetables or teaching methods either as result of work pressures or by choice.

But the arrival of the internet has catalysed distance learning and enhanced its appeal greatly. The increased potential for interactivity coupled with the added convenience of having resources to hand on your desktop, makes it far more exciting for education providers and students. Not only can you access comprehensive databases of the world's distance-learning institutions, but increasingly digital textbooks and other learning resources are being developed for online users. The internet has broadened the range of opportunities for students massively by making foreign courses more accessible, too. You can study any time, anywhere in this new global education marketplace.

As mentioned above, however, unqualified organisations can set up online distance-learning courses very easily, so would-be learners should approach any course provider with caution. You should also try to find out from friends, relatives, teachers, professors or work colleagues as much as you can about the standing of the institution you're interested in. As the number of online learning opportunities multiplies, the danger is that academic credibility is diluted.

Here are some of the leading proponents in the field of distance-learning courses, plus some information resources to help you find out more about the subject and which institutions have a better reputation than others. Bear in mind that the internet is both a resource for finding out about courses, whether online or offline, and a way of *delivering* those courses. The websites listed below offer one or both of these functions.

WARNING

Unqualified organisations can set up online distance-learning courses very easily, so would-be learners should approach any course provider with caution.

Learndirect (www.learndirect.co.uk)
Learndirect is the government's initiative to encourage lifelong learning throughout the nation, to create a better qualified, better educated and more competitive workforce.
It set up the University for Industry (Ufi) to oversee the project. Ufi is a public-private partnership operating in England, Wales and Northern Ireland whose chief aim is to help people get jobs and improve their career prospects. More than 80% of the courses on offer are online, but there are also 900 Learndirect centres where people can go if they don't have access to a computer. Most of the course materials can be found online, otherwise workbooks,

Learndirect is the government's attempt to encourage us all to continue our education right through life, with thousands of courses on offer (www.learndirect.co.uk). Learn online or visit a Learndirect centre if you prefer the personal touch.

CD-ROMs and videos can be sent to your home address. The aim is to make learning as flexible and as easy as possible. For the Scottish version of the site go to www.learndirectscotland.com.

The International Centre for Distance Learning (ICDL) (www.icdl.open.ac.uk)

This is an amazingly comprehensive resource from an international centre for research, teaching, consultancy, information and publishing activities that is part of the **Institute of Educational Technology** (/iet.open.ac.uk). ICDL's distance-learning databases contain information on some 31,000 programmes and courses mostly in the Commonwealth countries, more than 1,000 distance-learning institutions worldwide, and over 12,000 abstracts of books,

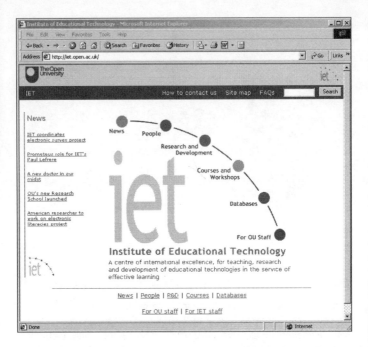

A huge resource of distance-learning courses worldwide, the International Centre for Distance Learning is part of the Institute of Educational Technology (iet.open.ac.uk).

journal articles, research reports, conference papers, dissertations and other types of literature relating to all aspects of the theory and practice of distance education. You can search easily in a number of ways to pinpoint the type of course you're interested in and the right institution to provide it.

Open and Distance Learning Quality Council (www.odlqc.org.uk)

This is an independent charitable organisation set up more than 30 years ago to monitor the quality of distance-learning providers. It offers a 'rigorous' vetting and accreditation scheme and the site lists all the colleges it has accredited. There are links through to these colleges plus a list of all the courses they offer. You won't find too many degree courses here though – they're mainly business and professional skills courses. If you're concerned about the quality of online learning providers, this is a very useful starting point.

The National Extension College (www.nec.ac.uk)

The Cambridge-based NEC is a non-profit-making trust set up to provide educational opportunities for all, not just those who got the right grades. It caters for around 20,000 students a year and there are 140 courses offered, including 26 GCSE subjects, 23 A-level subjects, and degrees from the University of London. There are also various vocational qualifications and business skills courses to pursue. It is accredited by the Open and Distance Learning Quality Council (*see above*).

Open Learning Centre International (www.olc.ac.uk)

Open Learning Centre International (OLCI) is a kind of forerunner to the current government's 'learndirect' initiative with the emphasis on training and development for industry, commerce and public organisations. It was set up by the Manpower Services Commission in 1983 and now boasts students from more than 90 countries worldwide. It is accredited by the Open and Distance Learning Quality Council. The site itself is a garish yellow and feels quite amateurish compared to others in the same field, but the list of courses is comprehensive.

MindEdge (www.mindedge.com)

This is a slick US site set up by education professionals from Harvard and Massachusetts Institute of Technology. It is designed to be a one-stop-shop search facility for anyone interested in learning, whether online or via more traditional

A one-stop shop for a wide range of courses available internationally (www.mindedge.com), including distance learning, online study and more traditional methods. When you find a course you like, you can register online too.

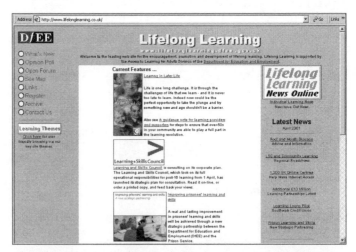

Why stop learning after college? This DfEE site (www.lifelonglearning.co.uk) encourages people to continue their education right through life, and tells you just what the government's doing to achieve it. Is there no escape?

methods. It encompasses distance learning, continuing education and business training courses both in the USA and internationally. But the site isn't just a directory, it offers online pre-registration of courses, links to bookshops and other relevant retailers, chat rooms for students, and online advice.

Lifelong Learning (www.lifelonglearning.co.uk)
This is a site set up by the Department for Education and Employment specifically to promote continued education throughout life. There's a collection of links to news about various lifelong learning initiatives the government has begun.

Online universities

A bricks-and-mortar university having a website is one thing, but a purely 'virtual' university is quite another. It has to be said that the concept is furthest advanced in the USA, where the huge distances some students have to travel make the advantages of the internet more appealing. Although online universities obviously come under the heading of 'distance learning', it is important to stress that they are on a higher academic level than those online academic institutions offering mainly vocational courses. Some, like the Open University listed below, are hybrids, incorporating online and distance learning with occasional face-to-face tutorials on campus.

E-University (www.hefce.ac.uk)
You can find out the latest news about the government's plan to establish an e-University at the site of the Higher Education Funding Council for England, which is co-ordinating the project. Progress is being made more rapidly than expected

Discover what the government's plan for an e-university is all about, with the website from the snappily entitled Higher Education Funding Council for England (www.hefce.ac.uk).

after a majority of higher education institutions expressed broad support for the concept following consultation. The idea is to develop a high-quality virtual learning centre by encouraging colleges and universities to take part, and to submit ideas and courses. In March 2001 the Council was in the process of shortlisting private sector partners for the project, as is the current vogue. The government has committed £62 million over three years for the e-University and we may even see a launch before the end of 2001. Go to the e-University section of the website if you want to find out more about the business model, read the consultation comments, or follow the latest developments.

The Open University (www.open.ac.uk)

The Open University is the UK's largest university with
around 200,000 part-time and full-time higher education
students taking its courses. It started out in 1971 and is
probably best known for its TV programmes shown in the
early hours of the morning presented by those notorious
beardy scientist types wearing woollen ties. As you might
expect, the internet complements the OU's distance-learning
objectives very well. Around 40,000 students study
interactively online. You can find out all about the
undergraduate and postgraduate courses on offer, with advice
on which course would suit your abilities and expectations.
And you can request a prospectus and reserve a place on a
course online. With the advent of high-speed 'broadband'

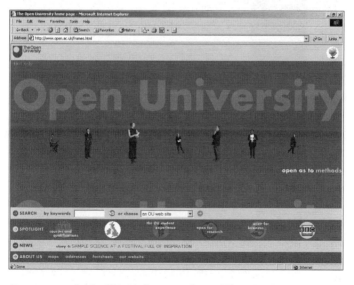

*For many people, the OU simply means obscure TV programmes at
4am but you can find out all about the UK's most famous distance-
learning institution on this site (www.open.ac.uk) – at any time of the day
or night.*

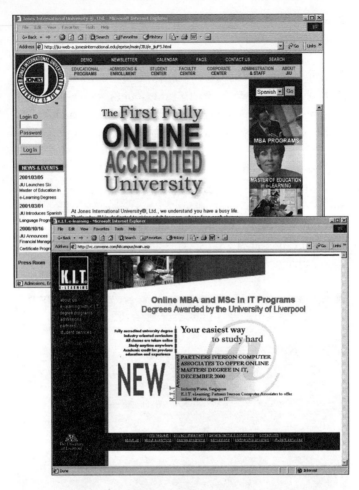

It is now possible to study for graduate and postgraduate degrees online.
Jones International University, based in the USA, claims to be the world's
first fully online accredited university, offering a variety of degrees in various
subjects, all administered on the web (top, jiu-web-a.jonesinternational.edu/
eprise/main/JIU/ e_jiuFS.html).The UK's first internet-only MSc and MBA
courses are now available (bottom, vc.convene.com/kitcampus/main.asp):
even the testing is done online.

internet connections it is likely that the online interactive element will increase, with OU TV programmes being downloaded on to PCs. No more setting the video and then hogging the TV while the rest of the family want to watch their favourite soap. Until then, you can find out what OU programmes are on the BBC by clicking through to a dedicated site, **Open2.net** (www.open2.net).

University of London External Programme (www.london external.ac.uk)

As the website so pithily puts it: 'If you can't come to London to study then London can come to you'. The University of London offers a wide range of diplomas and degrees online, targeted mainly at overseas students, with syllabuses and course materials available online. The University promises no drop in the usual standards of its qualifications, but there is no tuition offered. All papers are marked in London.

Unext (www.unext.com)

A US online university set up by leading academics initially targeting the global business market by offering employee training and business courses online. It has cracked the credibility problem by signing leading US institutions, such as Stanford, the University of Chicago and Columbia Business School, as well as the UK's London School of Economics. It calls its online university Cardean. Once you've registered you can browse the course catalogue. If the concept proves a success, there are plans to extend the range of courses to humanities subjects, too.

K.I.T. e-Learning (vc.convene.com/kitcampus/main.asp)

Founded in early 2000, K.I.T. e-Learning is a Dutch company, based in Rotterdam. It has developed the UK's first internet-only Masters Degree (MSc) in Information Technology and

Master of Business Administration (MBA), in collaboration with Liverpool University. The entire degrees are taught and tested online.

Jones International University (jiu-web-a.jones international.edu/eprise/main/JIU/e_jiuFS.html)
This US university claims to be the world's first fully online accredited university, offering MBAs, BAs and other higher education qualifications in a variety of subjects. Everything that students need is available online.

Chapter 6

Safety Online

Introduction

Safety is, of course, high on the agenda when it comes to children using the internet. It is not just pornography you have to watch out for either. There are many other unsavoury sites out there, from violence and racism, to just sick jokes. Even putting innocuous words in a search engine can elicit shocking results. In this chapter we look at arming yourself against the worst the internet can throw at you. We tell you about anti-virus software that can protect your computer against malicious viruses and about internet filtering programs that block sites you don't want your kids to have access to. We also show you how to arrange for your kids to surf in safety within secure 'walled garden' environments. There's advice for teachers setting up school websites, and general advice on how to use computers safely.

Internet security constantly recurs as a major concern of parents and teachers wanting to make the most of the internet, but worried that they may be exposing their children to possible harm. This chapter aims to put such fears to rest.

Using computers safely

If you are buying a computer and setting up internet access at home or at school for the first time there are some basic, common sense rules you should follow to make sure kids come to no harm.

1. Make sure children don't sit too close to the screen as it could strain their eyes after prolonged use. Change the font size on screen to make text easier to read if necessary. You can also change the brightness of the screen image to prevent eye strain.

2. To prevent back and neck strain ensure that users adopt a good posture while sitting at the keyboard. This means keeping a straight back and positioning the screen so that the head can be kept fairly level with it.

3. When typing there should be support for the wrists to prevent Repetitive Strain Injury-type problems and hands should be cupped as if playing the piano. RSI cases are on the increase, although there are relatively few involving children.

4. Establish a family or school code of conduct outlining when and how computers are to be used.

Anti-virus software

Every single internet-enabled computer should have anti-virus software installed as a matter of course. This should be as obvious and natural as wearing a seatbelt in a car. Although there has been a lot of hype about viruses, with some juicy scare stories making the headlines, the fact is that most viruses are actually hoaxes. Whilst there are potentially dangerous viruses out there, they shouldn't cause any problems if you keep your software regularly updated.

With the rise of e-mail, viruses and other malicious programs have been able to hide inside messages or tag along as attachments. Basically, whenever anyone sends you a document or file, or you download files from the internet, you should make sure that your anti-virus software is capable of scanning it first. As new viruses are being created on a daily basis by egotistical computer nerds, it is essential that you keep

NOTE

Although there are potentially dangerous viruses out there, they shouldn't cause any problems if you keep your software regularly updated.

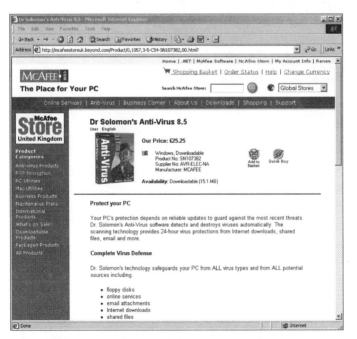

Protect your PC from viruses with one of the anti-virus programs available, such as Dr Solomon.

your programs updated. You can do this quite easily by regularly visiting the website of the product provider and downloading the latest database file listing all the most recent nasties that have been discovered.

There are three main packages to choose from, each costing around £30. Updates are usually free for a year after purchase. They are

Dr. Solomon's Home Guard   **www.drsolomon.com**
McAfee VirusScan (now part
   of Network Associates)   **www.nai.com**
Norton AntiVirus   **www.symantec.com**

If you buy a new computer with anti-virus software pre-installed (as is common these days) do check straightaway with the software manufacturer that you have the latest version and the most up-to-date virus detection file, sometimes called the signature file or virus definition file.

Filtering internet content

It must be said right at the start that there is no infallible way of protecting your children from accessing web pages you'd rather they didn't see other than monitoring their internet use constantly. The web filtering packages discussed below, whilst a significant addition to security, should not be relied on entirely. They are not perfect yet. Part of the problem is that one person's idea of pornography, blasphemy, violence, or antisocial behaviour may not be another's. There are not many agreed content standards around, and those that exist can seem pretty blunt instruments at times. Rules applicable to one age-group of internet users, may not be applicable to another age-group. Parents and teachers have to adopt a flexible, yet hands-on, approach to security at all times. You can't just rely on the software.

Here are some security strategies. Firstly, it is possible to set passwords for your computer so that no-one can get access without you being there. Secondly, you could supervise all online activity and surf the web with your children. Thirdly, before we even get to the filtering software, bear in mind that both leading internet browsers now incorporate their own security filtering features. Using a standard called Platform for Internet Content Selection (PICS), they allow you to select the level of content you are prepared to accept in four categories of language, sex, nudity and violence.

In Internet Explorer go to 'Tools', 'Internet Options', then click the 'Security' tab. In Navigator select 'NetWatch' under the 'Help' menu. One problem with these PICS settings is that they can be extremely sensitive. Set them to a moderate security level and you often find that you cannot

N O T E

Parents and teachers should adopt a flexible, yet hands-on, approach to security at all times.

access the most harmless-seeming of pages. Every time you try to access such a 'banned' page you'll be told you're not authorised to do so without entering the password. This can become extremely tiresome after just a few seconds, so some experimentation is definitely required.

There are various web filtering software packages on the market these days, typically costing between £30 and £40. Just to make things more complicated, they work in a number of different ways. Some allow you to create a list of allowed websites and ban all the rest, others simply filter out those sites on your banned list. Some work on the basis of spotting key words in web addresses, or images likely to contain nudity. Some packages combine all these filtering methods, allowing you to set them up in any way you want.

Cyber Patrol's software (www.cyberpatrol.co.uk) filters out unsuitable sites before your kids get to see them. Try before you buy with a free trial download.

Here is a list of the leading contenders in the web filtering market for homes and schools:

Cyber Patrol	www.cyberpatrol.co.uk
The Bair Filtering System	www.thebair.com
Bess Internet Filtering Service	www.n2h2.com/solutions/ school/school_products.html
Chaperon 2000 (C2K)	www.edu-tec.com
Cyber Sentinel	www.securitysoft.com
CYBERsitter	www.solidoak.com
Cyber Snoop	www.cyber-snoop.com
FamilyConnect	www.pornblocker.com
FamilyConnect 2000	www.cleansurf.com
I-Gear for Education	www.symantec.com/sabu/ igear/igear_educ
IF-NOT	www.turnercom.com/ifdir.html

KidDesk Internet Safe	www.edmark.com/prod/kdis
Net Nanny	www.netnanny.com
NetSweeper	www.net-sweeper.com/english
Planetweb Parental Control	www.planetweb.com/products/ web/pc.html
PureSight Education	www.puresight.net
RM SafetyNet Plus	www.rm.com/safetynet
SafeKids.Com	www.safekids.com
SafeSurf	www.safesurf.com
SurfControl	www.surfcontrol.com
We-Blocker	www.we-blocker.com
X-STOP	www.xstop.com

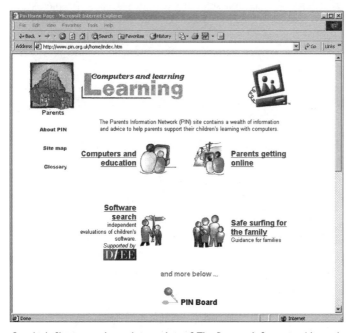

So which filtering package do you choose? The Parents Information Network (PIN) carried out an extensive review of the leading programs and you can check out their findings at www.pin.org.uk.

Choosing the best filtering package

With so many filtering options around, how do you pick the best? This depends largely on how you and your family use the internet, the age of your children, and how liberal you are about the language, images and other content they are allowed to see. No single solution is necessarily the best for everyone.

Luckily, there are some good reviews around to help you decide. For example the **Parents Information Network (www.pin.org.uk)**, an independent organisation set up to help parents use computers and the internet more effectively, carried out an extensive review of most of the leading packages. Its findings are summarised below:

1. There is no agreed standard way to solve the problems of monitoring and protection.

2. There is a huge variation in the rationale behind products and in the methods they offer.

3. No single product was found to combine all available filtering features.

4. There is no agreed quality standard of technical performance or user support.

5. When tested, most programs did not work as effectively as advertised.

6. Different kinds of families need different kinds of monitoring and protection and so must search for products that suit their needs.

7. Products need to be updated regularly to cope with changing patterns of internet use, changing content of websites and new ways to access online resources. None of them provides a permanent solution for parents.

The Consumers' Association magazine *Which?*
(www.which.net) also carried out a review of a selection of
filtering packages in its May 2000 edition. Significantly, not
one of the seven packages it tested successfully blocked all of
the sites that *Which?* chose in its experiment. This merely
adds weight to the view that such packages are only a partial
answer to the problem of internet security.

Always bear in mind that even the most sophisticated
filtering and monitoring software isn't going to deter the
most ingenious and persevering teenager from finding ways
around the security measures. And there is always the
danger that when something is forbidden it just becomes all
the more exciting and a greater challenge. Cod-psychology
aside, a combination of software and common sense should
guard your children against the worst excesses the net can
throw at us.

More filtering and safety advice

For more advice on the range of filtering tools available
and how to use them effectively, a US site called **GetNetWise**
(www.getnetwise.org) is worth a look. Also in the USA,
the Commission on Online Child Protection published a
report to Congress in October 2000 examining the various
ways that children can be protected online. For a more
in-depth look at these issues go to the **COPA Commission**
(www.copacommission.org). The European Union is also
devising its own Safer Internet Action Plan, featuring a
network of telephone hotlines to allow the reporting of
illegal internet content, investigation of filtering and rating
systems, and education of the internet's potential and
dangers. Full details are available at **Safer Internet**
(europa.eu.int/ISPO/iap).

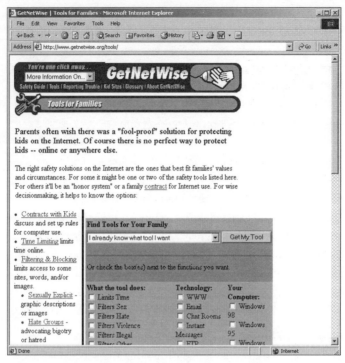

Get wise to the web by discovering filtering tools and how to use them at GetNetWise (www.getnetwise.org).

The 'walled garden' approach

If you're not happy with the level of security offered by web filtering software, you could go one step further and restrict access to a pre-selected list of websites. Once inside this 'walled garden' kids theoretically can't gain access to the world wide web. There are several ways these walled gardens can be operated, from CD-ROMs containing all the web pages – so in effect it's just educational software – to tailor-made web browsers that allow access only to the vetted list of sites and no others.

Some internet service providers will carry out the selection themselves, others will allow the parent or teacher to modify the list. In some versions, those in possession of a password can leapfrog the wall and gain unrestricted access. This way, users of all ages can make the most of the internet.

Walled gardens offer several advantages. Firstly, they are very secure. Once inside you can be pretty sure that young children won't be able to gain access to unsuitable material – providing you trust the product provider's choices! This means that internet usage doesn't have to be monitored. Secondly, they are very easy to set up – there are none of the complex adjustments that are usually required with filtering software.

But walled gardens have their limitations, too. They are only as good as the quality of sites selected. They don't actually teach older children how to surf the web responsibly and safely. And once the child has outgrown the level of the pre-selected sites, the walled garden ceases to have any appeal.

Also, a sophisticated child could easily skirt around the walled garden – by opening an alternative web browser, for example, and searching for inappropriate material via a search engine. Increasingly, search engines and directories are incorporating their own safety features, such as password requirements for adult-orientated searches. Others are restricting their web page databases to child-friendly websites. But as with filtering software, even the walled garden approach isn't necessarily 100% safe.

Below are some examples of walled garden services. However, be warned that some of the more commercial services listed will include adverts. Some parents may find such intrusions unpalatable.

Grid Club for Kids (www.gridclub.com)

The first rule of Grid Club is that everyone should talk about Grid Club. It's an out-of-school club designed to be a safe environment where kids aged seven to 11 can interact with each other, play games, and get help with homework and revision. It is a DfEE-funded project, admittedly still in its infancy, but with great potential. Safety is assured because the clubs the children belong to are hosted within a protected environment at Think.com, created by Oracle, the US computer systems giant. The clubs are run by club leaders who look after the children and monitor all the written communication. Every child who wants to be a member of Grid Club has to obey the club rules.

Control your kids' viewing at source with a filtering ISP such as @kidz (www.atkidz.com). Here they can chat online safely, have controlled access to e-mail and get help with their homework without fear of nasty surprises.

KZuk.net (www.kzuk.net)

This free UK ISP is purely for families with children aged between four and 12 years. Its internet access service incorporates security features, plus it offers a CD-ROM filled with some 20,000 pages of 'interactive fun and educational content' that can be read only offline. Parents can give older children password-protected access to the internet that is governed by NetNanny filtering software.

@kidz (www.atkidz.com)

Another controlled ISP service involving CD-ROM software, @kidz provides controlled access to e-mail and online chat for kids, plus homework help and educational fact files.

AT Kids Browser (www.winshare.com/mkbindex.htm)

A multimedia web browser that provides an education-oriented filtered environment for children to surf the internet.

ChiBrow (www.chibrow.com)

Another dedicated web browser designed for children, which parents can program to define which sites their offspring have access to.

AngliaCampus (www.angliacampus.com)

Content service developed from Anglia Interactive and CampusWorld services.

BT Talk21e (www.talk21e.com)

British Telecom's web-based service tailored for the schools market.

Edex (www.edex.net.uk)

This internet service provider offers controlled access to the internet.

*Child-safe content services and ISPs such as www.angliacampus.com (top)
and www.edex.net.uk (centre) give parents the confidence to let their
children surf the internet, while educational e-mail packages like EasyMail
from RM (bottom, primary.rm.com) help kids to learn in safety as they
post their electronic messages around the world.*

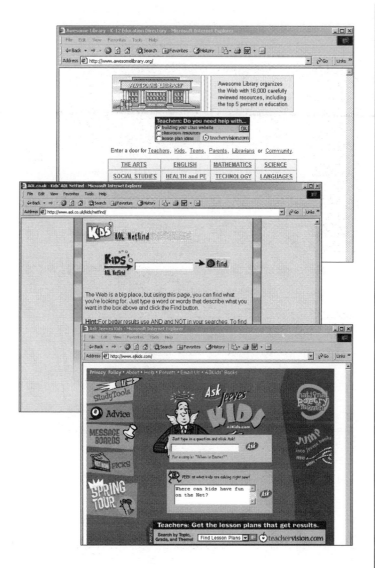

The Awesome Library (top, www.awesomelibrary.org) contains more than 14,000 educational resources for kids, all reviewed by librarians. AOL's family-oriented ISP has a browser (centre, www.aol.co.uk/kids/netfind) that allows parents to set different security levels depending on which family member is using the internet. Ask Jeeves For Kids (bottom, www.ajkids.com) is a great child-friendly version of the Ask Jeeves search engine.

RM EasyMail Plus (www.ifl.net/easymailp/index.html)

An educational e-mail package incorporating security measures.

AOL Net Find Kids Only (www.aol.co.uk/kids/netfind)

The world's largest ISP has made great play of its child- and parent-friendly environment. As AOL offers its own browser to members it can offer more control over what children are allowed to see. Its Parental Controls section allows adults to set a security level for each person who uses AOL.

Ask Jeeves for Kids (www.ajkids.com)

A search engine tailored to find child-friendly sites only.

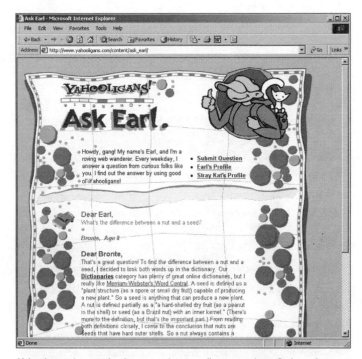

Yahooligans (www.yahooligans.com) is a really eye-catching, funky web directory for kids, courtesy of the world's largest portal Yahoo!

Awesome Library (www.awesomelibrary.org)
Over 14,000 librarian-reviewed resources for kids.

KidsClick (http://sunsite.berkeley.edu/kidsclick!)
More librarian-vetted websites for kids.

Kid's Search Tools (www.rcls.org/ksearch.htm)
A meta-search engine allowing kids to search using several child-friendly search sites.

SmartZones (www.edview.com)
A collection of an amazing seven million teacher-reviewed web pages.

Yahooligans! (http://yahooligans.com)
Another tailored web directory from the world's largest search portal Yahoo!

Safety in chat rooms

There has been a great deal of justified concern over internet chat rooms and the potential dangers they pose for children. These are places on the web where people can swap messages almost instantaneously with other people in the 'room'. You can either talk to everyone publicly or switch to one-to-one chat mode with anyone in the room. They're immensely popular and mostly harmless fun. A Home Office report published in March 2001 found that of the five million British children who use the internet, more than one million do so in around 100,000 chat rooms around the world.

But there is very little monitoring or policing of these chat rooms, so youngsters can easily be drawn into conversations of an overtly sexual or offensive nature. And it is very easy for chatters to assume a false identity and tell lies. This has led to notorious cases of paedophiles preying on children and cyber-stalkers harassing people generally.

There has been so much concern about this that the Internet Crime Forum, a group including representatives from the Association of Chief Police Officers, child welfare groups, internet companies and the Home Office, has recommended that protected children-only chat rooms be set up. These would be monitored by specially trained staff skilled at spotting inappropriate or sexually explicit language. Requests for meetings would also be closely scrutinised and vetted sites would carry recognisable safety 'kitemarks'.

Despite the laudable aims of the Internet Crime Forum, doubts must surely remain about any organisation's ability to police so many messages relayed in real time, although such moves must be viewed as a step in the right direction. For the time being then, parents and teachers should educate children about the potential dangers of chat rooms, much as they would about accepting lifts from strangers.

The following advice applies:

1. Never give out contact information such as your e-mail address, phone number, home or school address to people in chat rooms.

2. Never agree to meet someone unless you are absolutely sure who it is.

3. If you do agree to meet someone, do so accompanied by a responsible adult.

As mentioned elsewhere, the only sure way to protect children is to monitor their internet use completely.

Safety advice for teachers setting up school websites

There are many advantages to having a school website. Publishing costs are reduced radically because you can do away with the traditional school magazine. All those grainy black-and-white photographs of barely recognisable grim-faced hockey teams can be replaced by high-quality graphics thanks to high-definition colour digital scanning. Photos can be uploaded on to a website very easily and news and reports can be kept up-to-date. Parents with online access can feel more involved in the school's activities and perhaps more committed as a result.

In November 2000, the British Educational Suppliers Association estimated that 35% of primary schools and 75% of secondary schools now have school websites. Photos of pupils doing all the things that pupils do can engender a sense of pride and motivate them to achieve more.

But teachers have to be aware that the internet is an open medium and as such anyone, not just your target audience, can see what you're doing. In this age of near-obsessional concern about paedophiles, protecting children from dangerous characters is essential. The level of consideration for security has to be that much higher for online publishing, compared to traditional publishing, simply because it is so much more accessible.

The Department for Education and Employment (www.dfee.gov.uk) has issued guidance to teachers developing school websites. Below is a summary of the main points. For the full text go to safety.ngfl.gov.uk/document. php3?PG=9.

- Establish a clear policy with regard to the online use of photos of pupils and ensure support for this policy from governors, teachers and parents.

2 Don't use first names and family names of individuals in a photograph. Conversely, if you do name a pupil, don't use their photograph.

3 Seek parental permission to use a photo of a pupil so that parents are aware of the way the image of their child is representing the school.

4 If you want to use images, use pictures of things they've made, or excerpts from their written or art work. This allows you to show off their talents – and the quality of the school – without increasing the risk of inappropriate use of images of pupils.

5 Only use images of pupils in suitable dress.

6 Establish a recognised procedure for reporting the use of inappropriate images to reduce risks to pupils.

Who's in charge of the net?

Well, no-one really. For the purists out there, that's its beauty. It embodies the principles of free speech in their purest form. For others it appears to be a chaotic nightmare, a haven for the depraved and the psychopathic. The techies who charted the net's rise from humble, innocent beginnings in the seventies, see the rise of rampant commercialism on the web as a sad diminution of its ethos of free exchange. In the USA, home to the world's most dedicated conspiracy theorists, the net is often portrayed as the last truly free place on earth, in an age increasingly dominated by governmental and commercial surveillance of all aspects of our lives.

It many ways it *is* a strong force for democracy and freedom of expression. Tibetan monks, persecuted by Chinese occupying forces, have often used the net to communicate with the rest of the world, as have other downtrodden minorities. As a breathtakingly powerful tool for mass communication, the net can empower people by giving them information that they may not have been able to get hold of before. More than any other technological development it has shown that information is power.

So the net is still largely self-regulating, with businesses and service providers working out amongst themselves how best to deal with problems of security and authenticity. Although governmental interference is not welcomed by the net industry, the need for businesses to find common security standards to facilitate e-commerce has led to an inevitable increase in the part that governments have to play. The web is transforming economies now, not just helping academics to swap ideas.

There is a constant battle between the libertarians and those who would regulate the net far more tightly, citing the ubiquity of pornography and other obscene or antisocial content to bolster their case. The problem is that as the net expands to become a global phenomenon, reaching Communist countries as well, Western ideas concerning freedom of speech don't go down too well.

Generally governments have been happy to sit and watch developments, seeing how far existing legislation can be stretched to cover online activities. For the most part, the web is just another publishing medium. So existing laws to do with libel, for example, apply equally online as offline. But there are some unique problems, many of them to do with copyright. The web has made it very easy to copy and distribute images and sound in clear breach of copyright law.

Yet the net industry still believes technology will find solutions to these problems without the need for governments to impose cumbersome laws and potentially stifle business.

It is in the area of security that governments have made their presence felt. Law enforcement agencies generally want to retain the ability to open encrypted mail and get behind security firewalls when necessary in the name of national security. The UK government's recently passed Regulation of Investigatory Powers Bill allows it to do just that. Civil libertarians argue that such powers would be open to too much abuse.

While the debate rages on it will be up to parents and teachers to decide what balance to strike between freedom and censorship, protection and exposure.

7

Buying Online

Introduction

In this chapter we look at how you can buy educational materials online, such as learning software, books, CDs, toys and pencil cases. A lot of what we buy for our children can come under the heading of 'educational'. And the web is an excellent tool that enables us to shop around, compare prices and buy in a safe and convenient manner.

But many people still have concerns about giving out their credit card details over the internet. In fact, a survey conducted by MORI and published in March 2001 showed that 46% of 17 million people who currently have access the internet in the UK still believe that releasing credit card details is just too risky to make online shopping worthwhile.

The fact is that instances of fraud are rare and that buying online is much safer than ordering goods over the phone. For example, the Association of Payment Clearing Services (APACS) announced in the same month that plastic card fraud losses cost the UK banking and retail industries £292.6 million in 2000, but that estimated losses from internet and telemarketing transactions amounted to just £7 million. The spectre of online fraud is a myth.

If you're still not convinced, there are several online payment schemes around that do not involve you sending credit card details over the net at all. For more information, *see* **Alternative online payment systems**, *page 126*.

We show you how to shop around on the web, recommending good retail sites to try, and we explain how encryption works to hammer home the safety message. If you follow our safety advice you should be able to buy anything you like online without fear – and even pick up the odd bargain along the way.

Books, CDs and videos for kids

Books are ideal goods to buy online because you don't have to touch them or test them first. They're small and post easily. This is why books, CDs, videos and DVDs remain – along with software – the most popular items that people buy online.

Here are some online bookshops to try.

Alphabet Street	www.alphabetstreet.infront.co.uk
Amazon	www.amazon.co.uk
Blackwells	www.blackwells.co.uk
BOL	www.uk.bol.com
Bookpages	www.bookpages.com
Dillons	www.dillons.co.uk
Internet Bookshop	www.internetbookshop.co.uk
Waterstone's	www.waterstones.co.uk
W H Smith	www.whsmith.co.uk

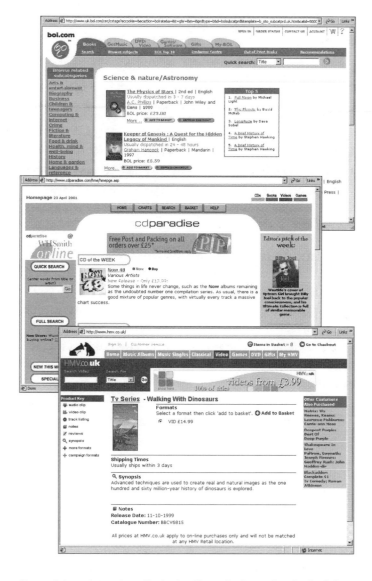

Some of the websites that offer books, CDs and videos online: Books Online (top, www.uk.bol.com), CD Paradise (centre, www.cdparadise.com) and HMV (bottom, www.hmv.co.uk).

For CDs, videos and DVDs try:

101CD	www.101cd.com
Amazon	www.amazon.co.uk
Blackstar (video and DVD only)	www.blackstar.co.uk
CD Paradise	www.cdparadise.com
Entertainment Express	www.entexpress.com
HMV	www.hmv.co.uk
Virgin Megastore	www.virginmega.com
Yalplay	www.yalplay.com

Toys and computer games for kids

Play is an important part of education, especially for younger children. Toys can help stimulate the imagination and teach co-ordination, logic and problem solving. There are lots of interesting toy shops around, so have fun browsing the online catalogues.

Dawson & Son	www.dawson-and-son.com
Early Learning Centre	www.elc.co.uk
Funstore	www.funstore.co.uk
Gameplay.com	www.gameplay.com
Games Paradise	www.gamesparadise.com
Hamleys	www.hamleys.co.uk
Internet Gift Store	www.internetgiftstore.co.uk
Jungle.com	www.jungle.com
Lego	www.lego.com
PlayBug	www.playbug.com
Shop4Toys	www.shop4toys.co.uk
Toys R Us	www.toysrus.co.uk
Toyzone	www.toyzone.co.uk

Rather than fighting your way through hordes of kids, order toys and games from the peace and quiet of your own home: www.toysrus.co.uk (top) and www.hamleys.co.uk (bottom).

Shopping via education websites

Canny education portal sites have realised that parents and teachers want advice and guidance but also the chance to put that advice into practice. If you can read an online review of some educational software and then buy it on the same site, you're more likely to do so. The same goes for books and any other educationally relevant stuff. Below are just a few websites with e-commerce sections attached.

Schoolsnet (www.schoolsnet.com)
This site offers guidance and reviews on books for children of all ages, plus online shopping facilities thanks to a link

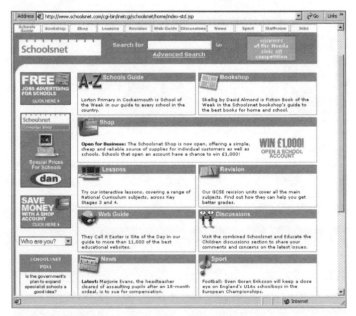

Where can you find the best books for your children? Schoolsnet (www.schoolsnet.com) offers guidance for all age groups, plus a link to Amazon.co.uk once you've made your choice.

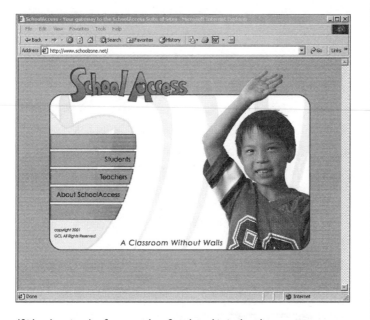

If it's educational software you're after then this is the place to come. Schoolzone (www.schoolzone.net) has links to 30,000 educational resources all reviewed by teachers and available to buy online.

with Amazon.co.uk. In its main shop you can buy all sorts of things, from printing stationery to materials strictly relevant to the National Curriculum. Schools who register with the site can also buy computers from Dan, a leading manufacturer, at discount rates, and cut-price software from Microsoft through its Student Licence scheme.

Schoolzone (www.schoolzone.net)

Another excellent educational website, Schoolzone features links to 30,000 internet resources reviewed and categorised by UK teachers. So if you're looking for educational software to teach and entertain the kids with, check out the reviews here and the chance to order the products online. Definitely worth a look.

General shopping tools

If you just want to browse the hundreds of online retailers for interesting things to buy, you could try some of the shopping portal sites first. These are directories of retail websites, sometimes reviewed and rated. You can usually peruse the site's selection of special offers and make the most of the online buying advice.

Most leading internet service providers and search portal sites have shopping sections, too. Some will vet the sites first before admitting them into their shopping zones. Others also negotiate discounts from the retailers for their registered members.

Some of these shopping directories and portal sites incorporate price comparison agents that scour a number of retailers to track down the lowest prices for whatever you're looking for. These price comparison services are growing in sophistication. The results can often include the cost of delivery and even display the typical delivery time.

> **TIP**
>
> *Most leading internet service providers and search portal sites have shopping sections.*

Here's a selection of the best online shopping tools currently around.

ShopSmart (uk.shopsmart.com)

ShopSmart is a leading shopping directory incorporating reviews and ratings with an ever-expanding price comparison engine. You can look for the cheapest products in a number of categories, such as books, CDs, DVDs and videos. Definitely a site to bookmark and go to if you're ever planning an internet shopping spree.

Two handy sites offering price comparison engines: the shopping directory
ShopSmart (top, uk.shopsmart.com) and DealTime (bottom,
www.dealtime.co.uk).

Kelkoo (uk.kelkoo.com)

Another great shopping directory and price comparison engine, Kelkoo is constantly adding new categories to its website. For example, you can now look for the cheapest place to buy toys and mobile phones, as well as the usual books, CDs and so on. Bookmark this as well and you won't need much else.

DealTime (www.dealtime.co.uk)

This is an international price comparison engine with one of the most comprehensive lists of product categories I've seen on the web. One of its best features is the way it takes delivery costs into account when ranking the prices and its ability to display the prices in a currency of your choice, even if the sites are foreign. There are buying guides and special offers negotiated by the website.

BookBrain (www.bookbrain.co.uk)

As its name suggests, BookBrain sticks to books and does its job extremely well as a result. You can search by author, title, publisher or ISBN for books in the inventories of 14 UK online bookshops, making it unlikely that you'll miss the book you're looking for. What's more, you're almost certain to get it at the lowest available price thanks to the price comparison engine.

Virgin Net (www.virgin.net/shopping)

ISP Virgin Net has opted for quality rather than quantity, vetting its partner retailers and demanding discounts from them to offer its members. For example, retailers wanting a 'Virgin Recommends' tag have to agree to offer 5% cashback to Virgin Net members, as well as providing secure online ordering and delivery guarantees.

Egg Shopping (www.egg.com)

An internet banking website may seem an odd place for a shopping portal, but if you use Egg's credit card you get 2% cashback on goods bought from its selection of retailers. Egg also promises to reimburse anyone who is defrauded while shopping online using the Egg card.

Some other ISPs with shopping sections:

Yahoo UK	uk.shopping.yahoo.com
Freeserve	www.freeserve.net/shopping
Excite	www.excite.co.uk/shopping
Microsoft Network	www.msn.co.uk
LineOne	www.lineone.net
Zoom	www.zoom.co.uk
UK Max	www.ukmax.com/shopping

Many ISPs, such as Zoom (www.zoom.co.uk), are offering goods and services alongside internet access.

Secure online shopping

Not many people seem to believe it, but shopping online is actually safer than handing your credit card over in a restaurant or ordering over the phone. Most online retailers now offer secure payment systems that encrypt (*see* **How encryption works**, *opposite*) your credit details while they are in transit across the internet.

Despite this, the surveys still show that fear over security is still the main reason why people are reluctant to shop online. This fear is largely unfounded. And the best way of dispelling this fear is simply to do it and spread the word that the sky didn't fall in when you did.

But there are some security issues. More important than encryption is the security of the retailer's systems. There have been several cases of hackers being able to break into online retailers' systems, steal credit details, and publish them on the web. But how much should we worry about this? When we use our credit cards online, we are liable only for the first £50 of any loss due to fraud, so long as we haven't been negligent and we've reported any rogue purchases as soon as we discovered them. In a way, it's not our problem – it's the card providers' and the retailers' problem. Of course, it comes back to us in the long run. If the fraud losses mount, the cost is inevitably passed back to the consumers somewhere down the line.

WARNING

Debit cards do not enjoy the same level of protection under the law as credit cards, so if there is a choice of payment method on a website, always use your credit card.

The standard online payment security system is called Secure Sockets Layer (SSL), developed by Netscape for its Navigator web browser. Now it is the most widely used system and is supported by all the major browsers. There are other security systems around, such as the Secure Electronic Transaction (SET) protocol developed by Visa and MasterCard among others. The main advantage of SET is that the retailer can find out if the cardholder is using a valid card without needing to see the credit card details, and the card issuer doesn't know what is being bought, just the price.

Confidence in secure payment systems has grown to such an extent that several credit card providers now offer fraud guarantees with their cards, promising to stand any loss the customer incurs through fraud on the web.

Now that strong (128-bit – *see* **How encryption works**, *below*) encryption has become widespread and security of data crossing the net is assured, we should be able to buy things online in complete safety. But there is a growing number of alternative online payment mechanisms coming on to the market (*see* **Alternative online payment systems**, *page 126*), catering for security-conscious shoppers and those who may just want to be able to pay for things in any number of ways. One of the simplest is electronic funds transfer, where cash is taken directly from your bank account, as if paying with a debit card. This way there are no credit card details being transmitted at all. We'll also see 'electronic purses' that store electronic cash being used for smaller online purchases, where credit cards wouldn't be cost effective.

How encryption works

Your credit card details are pretty safe when crossing the web because they are encrypted, providing you're connected to a computer capable of handling encryption, known as a secure server. Encryption is a way of scrambling information so that it can be transferred across an open network, such as the net, without anyone being able to understand what the message is. Only the intended recipient has the 'key' to unlock the code. The data is jumbled up according to a mathematical formula or algorithm and the way these rules are implemented depends on a what's called a 'cryptographic key', made up of a variable string of ones and noughts called bits.

The standard form of encryption now available for consumers has a 128-bit key – this is very strong and enough to put off even the most determined of code-breaking fraudsters. So you don't need to worry. Anyway, the key to successful cryptography is not discovering a completely foolproof code, but making it so difficult that it's not worth anyone's while to try to decode it. As long as the value of the prize is lower than the cost of winning it, encryption should deter criminals. A criminal who can easily get your credit card number from a carbon paper receipt in a shop or restaurant is hardly going to bother linking up hundreds of computers on the off-chance that she or he might intercept your number as it whizzes through cyberspace.

The most widespread forms of encryption rely on a system of unique digital keys for encoding and decoding the data or messages. One of the by-products of this is that it is also possible to use encryption as a way of verifying the identity of the sender, and that the message or data hasn't been tampered with in transit. This may involve loading

TIP

Look for the sites that carry the following logos, guaranteeing a degree of reliability and services:

Webtrader

ImRG

TrustUK

digital certificates on to your computer that can then be used to encrypt messages going to those sites that own the certificates.

But for day-to-day shopping on the net, a simple secure server that scrambles your card and personal details before transit is quite sufficient.

Spotting retailers who offer secure payments

First of all the retailer will probably trumpet the fact very loudly. It wants more than anything for customers to feel that they can buy online in confidence. But don't just take its word – your browser will tell you. You will usually see a closed padlock symbol at the bottom of your screen, indicating that the site is secure. You may also see that the web address has changed so that the address begins **https://** rather than the usual **http://**.

Encrypting data takes a lot of computer resources and can slow things down considerably on the web, so what many online retailers do is give you the option of switching between secure and insecure mode. If you're just browsing the store and choosing things to buy, there's no reason for the link to be secure – you're not transmitting any sensitive information. It's when you come to buy using your credit card that you need encryption. So at this point retailers will often have a button giving you the option to switch to secure mode. This is when you should see the web address and the browser security icons change.

How to vet online retailers

Online shoppers do have legitimate concerns about shopping online, but they shouldn't be about using credit cards. The main problem is knowing who you're dealing with. If you've never heard of the site, how do you know that it's genuine, has the goods it says it has and will deliver them? How do you know that they will keep your credit card details secure from theft, internal or external? In short, you don't. You have to satisfy yourself about genuineness and reliability.

In the high street you'd be a little suspicious buying goods at knock-down prices from a bargain-basement shop. We all know what these places look like and we're pretty familiar with the hard sell patter. On the net it's easier to put up a sophisticated and credible shop front. Proving authenticity and integrity is a harder task for shoppers. Some fraudsters have passed themselves off as genuine retailers then gleaned the credit card details from gullible victims and gone on spending sprees using the stolen numbers. It is quite easy to make a website that is virtually identical to a well-known site.

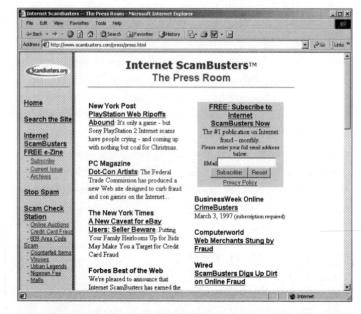

An in-the-know site offering inside information on the latest online shopping scams (www.scambusters.com).

Follow these simple rules to protect yourself:

① Never give your card details over the net except via a secure server.

② Never write down or disclose passwords, log-in names or Personal Identification Numbers (PINs).

③ Stick to well-known, well-regarded websites if possible. Ask friends for recommendations.

④ If you've never heard of a website and you're unsure about it, look for a physical address and a telephone contact number. Test them to establish that the business really exists. Ask your friends if they've heard of it. If you have any remaining doubts, don't deal with them.

⑤ Also check that the web address is exactly right. Fraudsters can sometimes set up virtual copies of well-known brand-name websites. A dot here and a hyphen there can make all the difference. And bear in mind that a .co.uk or .uk ending doesn't necessarily mean that the site is based in the UK.

⑥ Look for sites that have been given a 'kitemark' certificate by an accreditation scheme, such as VeriSign, WebTrader from the Consumers' Association, TRUSTe, BBBOnLine, TrustUK and JIPDEC. These schemes check out websites for authenticity, security, and responsibility in the handling of personal details.

⑦ Look for sites that send you an e-mail confirming your order and giving you a unique order number that you can use to track the progress of your purchase. Make sure you keep these e-mails as proof of purchase and for reference if you need to contact the retailer.

⑧ Ask what delivery guarantees an online retailer gives and what its returns policy is. If it is a UK site you're covered by normal consumer law, such as the Sale of Goods Act, and entitled to a full refund if goods are faulty or not as advertised. Be extra vigilant when ordering from abroad because UK law doesn't apply.

⑨ If you're dealing with a financial product provider, check that it is fully authorised for its range of activities. You can check the company against the **Financial Services Authority's central register** (www.thecentralregister. co.uk).

⑩ If a website is offering something that looks too good to be true, it probably is. Treat it with extreme caution. For news on the latest net frauds and scams try sites such as **Internet Fraud Watch** (www.fraud.org) and **Internet ScamBusters** (www.scambusters.com).

⑪ Use a credit card to pay online. The card issuer is obliged to refund you under Section 75 of the Consumer Credit Act if the goods fail to arrive or are damaged.

Alternative online payment systems

Alternative payment systems tend to fall into two camps, involving either telephone billing or pre-pay solutions. Broadly speaking, phone billing involves online purchasers being transferred to premium-rate telephone numbers whilst accessing the data or services they're paying for. The cost of the transaction appears on the telephone bill.

There are also several 'pre-pay' schemes that work in much the same way as pre-pay mobile phone cards. You just enter in the card's code number when making a purchase and the value is debited accordingly from your card. One major advantage of pre-pay schemes is that parents can allow their kids to shop online without having to resort to the parental plastic. Electronic cash cards can be slotted into card readers that plug into your computer when you want to go shopping. This can give a child the freedom to make his or her own purchasing choices without the risk of breaking the bank. With some schemes you don't even need cards at all; the cash is software-based.

Below are some companies offering alternative online payment systems.

SafeDoor (www.safedoor.co.uk)

UK security company Securicor is trying to extend its 'real world' reputation to the virtual world with its SafeDoor service. Shoppers worried about divulging credit card details over the web can set up an account with SafeDoor, registering their card details with the company once over the phone. That is the only time they have to divulge card details to anyone. They then shop online via the SafeDoor site at participating retailers, such as **101CD (www.101cd.com)** and **ThinkNatural (www.thinknatural.com)**. At the time of writing SafeDoor aimed to have 40 retailers signed up by the end of March 2001. SafeDoor acts as a go-between taking on the risk of fraud itself. This means the retailer doesn't have to carry out any security checks, simply receiving an electronic confirmation of the order from SafeDoor. You can also shop online anonymously if you want and SafeDoor can even keep your delivery address secret if you prefer. The company claims that none of its customer service employees will have access to card details, removing what has unfortunately proved to be a major source of credit card fraud in the past.

127

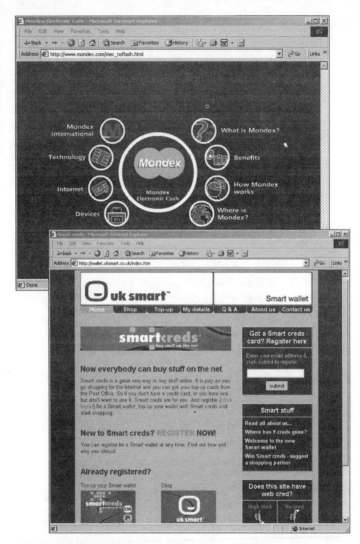

Reluctant to use your credit card online? Check out the alternatives from Mondex (top, www.mondex.com) and UK Smart (wallet.uksmart.co.uk/index.htm).

Other companies offering online payment systems include:

Mondex	www.mondex.com
Earthport	www.earthport.com
eVopay	www.evopay.com
eCharge	www.echarge.co.uk
Acquist	www.acquist.co.uk
Coulomb	www.coulomb.co.uk
Global Internet Billing	www.interactivcash.com
UK Smart	wallet.uksmart.co.uk/index.htm
PayPal	www.paypal.com

Index

A

animation 1, 17
anti-virus software 87,
88–90
art galleries 32–35

B

BBC 20, 23, 47, 52, 67
bookmarking 38–39
Bookmarks 7, 38–39
creating 38
organising 39
books, buying online 110
Boolean logic 10–13
British Library 35
British Museum 32
broadband connections 2, 6,
21, 83
bulletin boards 16, 56
bullying 42, 45
anti-bullying websites 45
buying online 109–129
safety tips 125

C

CDs, buying online 110–111
chat rooms 16, 72, 81,
103–104
advice 104
safety in 103–104
childcare 45–46
citizen information portal 26
colleges 70–72
guides to 71
online colleges 6, 69
computer games, buying
online 112
computer viruses 87, 88–90
computers, using safely 88
credit cards, using online 36,
109–110, 120–121, 126

D

debit cards, using online 120
degree courses 70, 79, 85, 86
Department for Education
and Employment *see* DfEE

DfEE 42–47, 49, 64, 98, 105
dictionaries 28–31
diploma courses 70, 85
directories 4, 8, 9–16, 29, 36,
   37, 52, 55, 103, 116, 118
   definition 9
   list of 15
   safety features 97
   specialist directories 13
   using 9–16
directory enquiries 37
discussion groups 8, 16
distance learning 69, 70,
   75–81
   concerns about 69, 76

E
e-University 81–82
early years websites 57–63
education online
   introduction 1–6
   pitfalls 2
education portal websites 47,
   49, 51, 52–57, 64
   shopping via 114
education systems 47
   understanding 42
educational software 96, 114,
   115
electronic cash cards 127
encryption 120–123
   how it works 121–123
encyclopaedias 28–31

F
Favorites *see* Bookmarks
filtering software 3, 87,
   90–95, 96, 97, 99

filtering software (cont.)
   advice on using 95
   choosing 94–95
   list of packages 92
further education 69–86

G, H
government directory 26
government information
   24–28
high-speed connections 1, 6,
   21, 83

I
independent schools 49
internet 1
   as a learning tool 1, 5
   as a multimedia
      environment 1
   as a research tool 5, 10
   filtering content 90–95
   regulation 107
   who's in charge 106–108
internet service providers 17,
   116
   walled gardens 97, 99, 102

K, L
kitemarks 104, 125
libraries 31, 32–35
literacy guides 42, 55

M
magazines 8, 20
   list of 23
mailing lists 7, 8
meta-search engines 9, 13, 103
   list of 16
museums 32–35

N

national archives 27
National Curriculum 41–49,
    52, 54, 59, 64, 115
    guide to 45, 52, 64
National Grid for Learning
    25, 45, 64
National Statistics 28
Natural History Museum 33
news aggregators 23
news broadcasters 23
news resources 20–24
newsgroups 8, 13, 16–19
    list of 18
    posting messages 18–19
    vetting 16, 17
newspapers 8, 20
    lists of 23
newsreader program 17
numeracy guides 42, 56

O

OFSTED 28, 45
online retailers, vetting
    123–126
Open University 83–84

P

parent help sites 40, 41, 42,
    63
payment systems 126–129
posters 18
Public Record Office 27

R

radio 21
research resources 7–39, 43
    miscellaneous 36–37

resources for parents and
    teachers 6, 51–68
revision help 43, 51, 54,
    67–68, 98

S

safety 3, 6, 87–108
    advice 95
    and children 90–106
    in chat rooms 103–104
    in setting up websites
        105–106
    in using computers 86–90
    in using credit cards online
        120–126
school governor 49
school websites 41, 43, 87,
    105–106
    creating 54
    safety advice for teachers
        105–106
schools 41–49
    advice on choosing 43
    information on 47, 54
    performance data 41, 43
Science Museum 34
search engines 3, 4, 8, 9–16,
    19, 31, 36, 45, 102
    definition 9
    list of 15
    safety features 97
    the best 13–14
    using 9–16
searching 9–16
    advanced searches 12
    how to search 10–13
    tips 12

search portal sites 103, 116
secure payment systems 121, 123, 126
security 3, 87–108, 120–126
  and children 90–106
  in using credit cards online 120–126
  strategies 91
shopping directories 116
shopping online 109–129
  general tools for 116–119
  security 120–126
  via educational websites 114–115
shopping portal sites 116, 119
spam 18
special educational needs 49
students' websites 72–75

T
teachers' websites 56, 57, 64–65
teaching resources 51–68
technology news 24
testing in schools 45
thesauruses 28–31
threads 18
toys, buying online 112

U
universities 69, 70–72, 81
  applying to 68, 70

universities (cont.)
  guides to 71
  online universities 6, 81–86
Usenet 8, 13, 16–19
  accessing 17
  etiquette 19
  managing usage 17

V
video 1, 2, 17, 21
videos, buying online 110–111
virtual staffrooms 64

W
walled gardens 87, 96–103
  advantages 97
  e-mail packages 102
  examples of 98
  internet service providers 97, 99, 102
  limitations 97
  out-of-school club 98
  web browsers 96, 99, 102
web addresses 7, 16, 123, 125
  saving 38–39
  searching with 7
web browsers 13, 17, 38
  bookmarking in 38
  security features 91, 96, 121, 123
  walled gardens 96, 99, 102